YOU'RE MESSING WITH MY

COOL!

YOU'RE MESSING WITH MY COOL!

PLEZE RAYBON

Library of Congress Control Number: 2024910684

ISBN: 979-8-89228-155-3   (Paperback)
ISBN: 979-8-89228-156-0   (Hardcover)
ISBN: 979-8-89228-157-7   (eBook)

Printed in the United States of America

Snoopy is not happy with Jeff and Linda's work but they know too much. He orders Bryan and Roscoe to kill them.

                    SNOOPY
Bryan I want you, and Roscoe to get rid of Jeff and Linda. Take this syringe: - I want you to take Jerome with you. Make sure he sits in the front seat, and you set behind him. When you get close to Jeff's home, stick the syringe in his neck and he will be out in about five seconds. Take care of Jeff and Linda; then drag his ass in, and put the gun in his hand. Wait about ten minutes after you leave; then call Joe. (a dirty Cop) He should be just waking up when he gets there.

Bryan calls Jerome

                    JEROME JR.
(Ring...) What up Bryan?

                    BYRAN
Today is your lucky day: Snoopy wants to reward us for our hard work. We're going to come get you, then go by Jeff and Linda's place. Snoopy has something for us to do.

                    JEROME JR.
I will be ready!

They pick up Jerome, as they are riding along.

                    JEROME JR. (CONT'D)
          What kind of reward is Snoopy giving us?

                    ROSCOE
          I really don't know, - then he stuck
          Jerome in the neck with the syringe.

Jerome passes out. They go in and kill Jeff and
Linda. Then takes Jerome in, and puts the gun in
his hand.

                    ROSCOE (CONT'D)
          You can go get him now!

                    JOE
          We're close by, and we will take care
          of it.

They break in the door, and Jerome is just waking
up with a gun in his hand.

                    JOE (CONT'D)
          'Drop the gun'!!

                    JEROME JR.
          I don't have a gun!

                    JOE
          What's that in your hand?

With hands raised and still groggy; he Didn't
realize he was holding a gun. He looks up and see
the gun in his hand, drops it, and backs away.

                    JEROME JR.
          What the hell is going on?

                         JOE
      Look like you kill two people.

Jerome was sentence three years in prison, but
did only two years.

MASON FINDING OUT HE HAVE A TWIN BROTHER: TWO
YEARS LATER

Mason attends his mother's funeral, then onto the
cemetery. Mason standing there with tear filled
eyes as they lowered his mothers coffin into the
ground. Two days later Mason is reading some
papers he found in a box under his mothers bed,
and finds out he has a twin brother. They were
separated at a very young age, and his mother
never told him. He is hurt and confused.

NEXT DAY - MORNING

Mason is going to the only person who would know
the truth, his Aunt Joyce. Opening the door she
sees in his eyes that he knows, and before he
says anything.

                         JOYCE
        I'm so sorry Mason: but I promised Sarah
        that I would never say anything, -
        Mason, please believe me, that was the
        hardest thing I ever done!

                         MASON
        - But - there's so many questions, I
        don't know my father. I've never seen
        him. Is he still alive? Do anyone know
        where my brother is, and why did she
        give him away, instead of me?

                    JOYCE
I, I (Before she could finish her
phrase.)

                    MASON
(Began to show anger by rasing his voice.)
Do you know where my brother is, or my
father? Do you have any pictures, of
either of them?

                    JOYCE
Now you lower your voice young man!

                    MASON
- I'm sorry Aunt Joyce, - - - but do
you have any answers for me?

                    JOYCE
I have a picture of your dad when he
came home from...

                    MASON
My dad was in the military?

                    JOYCE
From prison.

                    MASON
Oh!

                    JOYCE
Your dad spent two years in prison for
something he didn't do. Your dad was
a good man.

                    MASON
    Was? - are you saying he's dead?

                    JOYCE
    No, I'm saying I haven't seen him in
    years.

                    MASON
    Well, can I see his picture?

                    JOYCE
    Yes, give me a minute to find my photo
    book.

She go's into a back room and returns with a photo
book. Sits next to Mason, and shows him a picture
of his mom, and dad together.

                    MASON
         So, this is my dad!

Staring at the picture with a smile on his face.

                    MASON (CONT'D)
    Why did they break up?

                    JOYCE
    Well, they were never married -

Mason looking at her with uncertainty.

                    JOYCE
    Mason - your dad was a pimp.

                    MASON
    What?!! - Was mama a...

                    JOYCE
No no! But that was why they didn't get
married, he didn't want to change; so
they went there separate ways.

                    MASON
Do you have a picture of my brother?

                    JOYCE
No.

                    MASON
Do you know who she gave him to?

                    JOYCE
She gave him to your dad, and he moved
to Philadelphia, and I haven't seen or
heard from them since.

                    MASON
    (Looking confused) Wow!!

                    JOYCE
What honey?

                    MASON
I mean - You would think they would
have kept in touch; that doesn't make
any sense to me. - Well, I guest I'm
going to Philadelphia. - It shouldn't
be to hard to find someone who looks
like me.

                    JOYCE
Oh no! He looks nothing like you, he
looks like his dad.

                    MASON
I will find them - what is my brother
name?

                    JOYCE
Jerome Jr., well it's obvious; that's
your dads name also.

HE THINK HE SO COOL - AFTERNOON

Jerome Jr. is now out of prison, He's Walking down
the side walk, dressed in a white tailored suite.
He has the coolest walk you ever seen, this guy
is styling. There are some young kids sitting on
there porch talking among themselves.

                    TONY
Look at him, he think he so cool, I'm
going to let the dog lose on him, I bet
that will mess with his cool.

When Jerome get about 20 yards from them

                    TONY (CONT'D)
Hey Mr.: You better run, that dog is
going to get you.

Jerome turns and see the dog, at first he's to
cool. Started out with his pimp run. - Now he's
in full stride.

                    JEROME JR.
Come on kids call your dog - this Shit
ain't funny.

The dog gets closer, and is gaining on him by the seconds. The kids are laughing so hard at him. Jerome jumps a fence,- now he's talking a lot of stuff.

                    JEROME JR. (CONT'D)
          If I ever catch one of you little punks
          out side your yard; I'm going to put my
          suedes up your ass. (Looking down at
          the dog) And for you! With your little
          four legged ass. If I had my revolver,
          I would give you some more spots; but
          they would be red.

Turning around to walk away, there are two Doberman pinscher standing in front of him licking their chops.

                    JEROME JR. (CONT'D)
          What the hell!!

Quickly looks around for an escape, sees a tree, and began running toward it, screaming at the top of his voice. Makes it to the tree, sitting on a limp, looking down at the dog that's standing on it's hind legs and the two front legs against the tree.

                    JEROME JR. (CONT'D)
          You are messing with my cool.

Music starts.

MASON COMES TO TOWN NEXT DAY - AFTERNOON

Mason comes into Philadelphia, driving a white two sitter convertible, BMW. He stops for a red light, while sitting there waiting for the light to change (Rico) a undercover cop dressed as a homeless person, coming from the opposite side of the street, walking real slow as though he's injured. By the time he gets in front of Mason the light changes. Rico is still taking his time crossing the street.

                    MASON
        Ah,- come on man, get your decrepit ass
        out of the way!

                    RICO
        Turns, and gives Mason the meanest
        look as he steps onto the curb.

                    MASON
        Stares back, and gives Rico the finger,
        and drives off.

Then he looks into his rear view mirror, and sees Rico running full speed toward him. The car in front of him is not moving fast enough, he's blowing his horn hoping the guy would speed up before the light turns red. But the light changed and the car in front of him stops and he can't go anywhere. (Without opening the door, Rico jumps in Mason's car).

                    MASON (CONT'D)
        Man you better get out of my car.

                    RICO
        Shut up!!

Mason frowns, but before he say any thing, Rico opens his jacket, and reveals a gun. Masons frown is replaced with a look of terror.

                    MASON
          Please Sir, I'm sorry for...

                    RICO
               (Not even looking at Mason)
          Oh, now I'm Sir! - I told you to shut
          up. - Now drive - I see you're from
          Chicago.

                    MASON
          Yeah.

                    RICO
          I guess you think you're pretty tuff huh.

                    MASON
               (Swiftly shaking his head from
               side to side.)

                    RICO
          I should make you pull into that ally
          and put a Philadelphia whipping on
          your punk ass. - what brings you to
          Philadelphia?

                    MASON
          I have a twin brother, whom I've never
          seen.

                    RICO
          What - you have a twin you've never
          seem!?

                    MASON
Yeah, we were separated at a very
young age; and I just found out about
him last week.

                    RICO
What is your brothers name?

                    MASON
Jerome.

                    RICO
Laughs.

                    MASON
Why are you laughing?

                    RICO
Well, the Jerome I know looks nothing
like you.

                    MASON
He...

                    RICO
Pull over in front of that bus stop.

Mason is wondering why Rico want to stop, he look
at Rico with a fearful look on his face.

Rico pulls a card out of his inner pocket, and
gives it to Mason.

                    RICO (CONT'D)
If you ever need any help, don't
hesitate to call me.
          (As he walks away he turns.)

Oh, be nice to the homeless.
(Then disappears into the crowd.)

Mason looks at the card that reads Sargent (Rico) undercover police.

MY DOGS TREED A BLACK MAN - AFTERNOON SAMEDAY

The old couple is peeping out of their window, honey call 911. She dials 911, and gives the phone to her husband.

                    POLICE
          Philadelphia's best, how may I help you.

                    OLD MAN
          Is this the Police?

                    POLICE
          Yes, how may I help you?

                    OLD MAN
          My dogs treed a black man.

                    POLICE
          What do you mean your dogs treed a
          black man?

                    OLD MAN
          I mean my dogs chased his black ass
          up a tree. He might be a criminal; you
          better get over here fast, I'm at 2425
          Elmwood Dr. Hurry!

POLICE
Someone will be there in a few minutes.

Minutes later the police are on the scene and they all know Jerome.

(One of the officers)
Jerome: what in the hell are you doing in these people's yard, up in a tree?

JEROME JR.
Them little punks over there; let their dog a lose on me, and I promise you, if I ever catch one of them little bastard out side their yard; I'm going to put a serious whipping on his ass. So you might as well lock me up now or later.

They don't want to lock him up because he's linked to their investigation.

THE OLD PIMP: JEROME SR.

Jerome Sr. He's walking into the barber shop and everyone is laughing, looking at the news. They turn and see Jerome, and everyone stop laughing. Now they are just staring at him; in fear, because they don't know how long he was standing there.

JEROME SR.
What are you guy's laughing at? (Then he sees Jerome Jr. Up in a tree) What in the hell is Jr., doing in that tree? (Looking around at everyone).

                    ONE OF THE BARBERS
He was trying to break into that house,
and got surprised by two Doberman
Pinschers.

                    JEROME SR.
Now!! - My boy might do a lot of things:
but breaking into someone's home, is
something he would never do, and I
would bet my life on it.

                    ONE OF THE BARBERS
Well, you tell us why he's in that tree.

                    JEROME SR.
Hell, I don't know; but I do know my son
would never do something like that!!

No one want's to piss Jerome off, so they remain
silent. And at that moment they show a taping of
the footage, and the reporter asking Jerome why
was he in that tree, and hearing his answer.

                    JEROME SR. (CONT'D)
I told you sons of bitches, my son
don't do that kind of crap!!

                    ONE OF THE BARBERS
I know you have heard the old saying;
the apple don't fall to far from the
tree.

                    JEROME SR.
What the hell that suppose to mean?
That was the purpose of the interview,
to prove his innocence.

(MORE)

                    JEROME SR. (CONT'D)
(Tilting his head and rasing his index
finger, to get their attention). I
might put my foot up a Negro's ass,
and talk about his mama; but you ain't
never heard of me doing stupid stuff.
Like breaking into someone's home or
sticking someone up!!

                    ONE OF THE BARBERS
Jerome, every since I've known you,
you've been a pimp!

                    JEROME SR.
That's true, but you can ask any of my
girls have I ever hit or misuse any of
them. The answer would be no!!

                    DENNIS
(Chuckling) They would probably be
afraid to say anything.
(Sitting in the chair getting a hair
cut). You got to be the oldest pimp I
have ever seen.

                    JEROME SR.
Refusing to reply to that statement,
walks over to the window and stares
out, looking at one of his girls.

                    DENNIS
What do his ladies look like?

                    ONE OF THE BARBERS
          Man! - Jerome got some fine ladies

                    DENNIS
          Yeah right! (Chuckling) they probably
          are some old hags.

Everybody who knows Jerome, is staring at him;
waiting for him to pull out his pocket watch, but
he seems to be ignoring the guy.

                    ONE OF THE BARBERS
          See that little pretty thing across the
          street, that's...

                    JEROME SR.
          Hey hey, don't be telling that young
          punk my business!!

                    DENNIS
          Really! - That girl standing right
          there, works for him? - (Turning toward
          Jerome) what would you do old man if
          she, or one of your girls come running
          to you and say,- 'will just say a guy
          like me, wouldn't pay them. What would
          you do, Call the police? - and how can
          someone kiss that yuck mouth? (Looking
          around at everyone laughing).

Finally Jerome looks at the guy - then reaches in
his pocket and pulls out his watch.

                    ONE OF THE BARBERS
          Oh Shit!!

                    DENNIS
Oh shit what?!!

Jerome looks at his watch, and walks out the door.

                    THE BARBER
All I can tell you young is, you better
get your ass out of here before Jerome
gets back.

                    DENNIS
What - he's going to get a gun or
something?

                    THE BARBER
No! Although you might wish you had
one. Now, if he comes back with some
boxing gloves; that means he really
don't want to hurt you. But if he's
wearing a white suit, that mean - well,
I wouldn't want to be in your shoes.

                    DENNIS
I just want...

                    THE BARBER
Let me finish: The reason he looked at
his watch is; it will take him about
five minutes to go home and change
cloths, and about two minutes to get
back.

                    (MORE)

                    THE BARBER (CONT'D)
He's going to give you three minutes to
apologize, and if you don't apologize -
He's going to use the other five minutes
whipping your ass. And I have been
told, those five minutes seem like an
hour.

                    DENNIS
So, what you are saying is; he's going
to either be wearing a white suit and...

                    THE BARBER
And if he's wearing a white suit, you
better get your ass out of here!!!

                    DENNIS
(Laughing) You say a white suit or
boxing cloves, and no gun right?

                    THE BARBER
Yeah, and I can tell you're not taking
me serious, so I'm through talking.

Jerome Jr. Is on his way to the barber shop,
seeing his dad crossing the street, he can tell
by the way his dad is walking someone has pissed
him off.

                    JEROME JR.
    Hey dad-

                    JEROME SR.
Not now son!!!

Jerome is hoping his Dad come out of those doors with a pair of boxing cloves. But two minutes later he came out wearing a white suit, and Jr. Knows he can't stop his dad when he's ready to fight.

The barber is looking out the window, and see Jerome wearing a white suit, turns and looks at Dennis.

> THE BARBER
> Man you better get the hell out of here, and quick!

> DENNIS
> (Walks over to the window and see Jerome), and bends over laughing.

> JEROME SR.
> (Walks through the door with his watch in his hand looks at it. All right young man, you have three minutes to apologize.

> DENNIS
> (Laughing so hard he can't get a word out. Trying to say, what are you going to do? But can only say) what, what (between laughs).

Everyone is laughing at Dennis, but Jerome is too pissed to laugh.

> JEROME SR.
> You got one minute to start apologizing, because after three minutes: I'm going to be on you like a bad odor.

Dennis is laughing so hard now he can't even stand up.

                    JEROME SR. (CONT'D)
          Get him out of here, it wouldn't be a
          fair fight.

Jr. Seeing them bringing Dennis out, is thinking his dad has really messed this guy up. Rushing into the shop.

                    JEROME JR.
          Dad, are you okay?

                    JEROME SR.
          Yeah!

                    JEROME JR.
          What happened?

                    JEROME SR.
          Nothing - that little punk wouldn't
          stop laughing. So I figured it wouldn't
          be a fair fight.

                    JEROME JR.
          Dad, that guy ain't no little punk,
          that guy can hurt you!!

Jerome Sr. looks out the window and sees Dennis talking to one of his girls.

                    JEROME SR.
          Well, I guess we're going see if the
          old man can still do it.

                    JEROME JR.
(Stepping in front of his dad). Dad
look at that guy: that guy can beat
both of us!!

                    JEROME SR.
Son I know you were in prison. You
didn't get cornholed did you? Now get
out of my way.

                    JEROME JR.
Cornhole? - but Dad listen to me, that...

                    JEROME SR.
Now you know I will knock your ass out,
to get to him. Now get out of the way.
(With a serious stare).

                    JEROME JR.
Steps a side, okay dad.

                    JEROME SR.
Walking across the street, gets right in
Dennis face. You're not going to laugh
your way out of this ass whipping...

                    DENNIS
Awe not you again; - Look here old man:
don't make me hurt you. My conscience
wouldn't let me sleep at night!

                    JEROME SR.
Well: - what if I put you to sleep.
(Knocking him out with a right to the
chin.

As Dennis is falling: everyone is saying with a loud voice "free fall, free fall", but instead he's reaching out, grabbing Jerome by the arm leaving a dirt stain on his sleeves.

                    JEROME SR. (CONT'D)
Awe hell no!!!

                    JEROME JR.
Dad lets get out of here before he wakes up!

                    JEROME SR.
I'm going to wake his ass up, you know I don't play that: he had a chance to make a clean fall. I even heard the guys from across the street, saying free fall. But this punk had to leave his finger prints on my sleeves, and that's a No no!!

                    JEROME JR.
Dad, come on!!

                    JEROME SR.
Jr. You got one more time to try and stop me: and I'm going to knock your ass out, you hear me.

                    JEROME JR.
(Knowing his dad will do it). Yes sir. (Stepping a side). I know I can't stop you dad, but that guy works for snoopy: and he might try to get revenge.

                    JEROME SR.
Do you want me to kill him?

                    JEROME JR.
No dad!!!!

                    JEROME SR.
Well, you better shut the hell up,
cause I ain't going to be looking over
my shoulders. I can take this punk out
right now!! - But I have to teach him
a lessen: so I'm going to wake his ass
up, and make sure he understand why
he got this ass whipping. Then knock
him out again for leaving his finger
prints on my sleeves. (Slapping him on
the cheek), wake your ass up!!

                    DENNIS
Moving his head from side to side -
What happen?

                    JEROME SR.
I knocked your ass out, that's what
happen.

                    DENNIS
Why did you do that, and what did you
hit me with?

                    JEROME SR.
If you answer a few questions for me
I will tell you. Now I know you were
getting your hair cut when I left. Now
when I was coming back to the shop, did
he tell you I was wearing a white suit.

                    DENNIS
Getting an attitude, stands to his
feet, you snuck that one in on me...

                    JEROME SR.
What's that I see in your eyes,- You're
trying get an attitude? - I ask you a
question.

                    DENNIS
Yes he told me you were wearing a white
suit, and yes I thought it was funny
as hell.

                    JEROME SR. (CONT'D)
Did He tell you when that old man
knot yo ass out to make a clean fall,
because if you touch and leave a smudge
on my suit how that would really piss
me off?

                    DENNIS
Yeah.

                    JEROME SR.
Then why did you...

                    DENNIS
Hey, hey enough with the questions. I'm
going to ask you one time, nicely. Old
man, get the hell out of my face.

                    JEROME SR.
Well that didn't sound to nice to me.

                    JEROME JR.
          Dad please, just...

Jerome is looking at Jr. With an evil eye.

                    JEROME SR.
          When I get through whipping his ass
          you better be gone. Because I have
          told you to never try to stop me, from
          beating some one that deserves a good
          ass whipping.

Dennis is so mad he grabs Jerome with both hands,
and slammed him against the wall.

                    DENNIS
          Look here old man I can brake every
          bone in body.

                    JEROME SR.
          That's what I'm talking about, if you're
          going to bring it, then bring it.

Dennis didn't know that Jerome was a 3rd degree
black belt. He was totally surprised with his
moves. The old man beat him down real good.

                    JEROME SR. (CONT'D)
          Looks at Jerome Jr. And start to run
          toward him, I told you...

                    JEROME JR.
          (Jerome Jr. Has this little pimp run
          that he learned from his dad) I was
          just worried about you!

                    JEROME SR.
You know what I can do! (Watching him
run like himself from behind he couldn't
stop laughing but still chasing him).

                    THE BARBER
I have never seem anything like
them two.

SAME DAY- I BELIEVE JEROME IS A SNITCH!

Mason is setting in a restaurant waiting for his
food. Two guys walks in talking about Jerome Jr.

                    BRYAN
Man I'm telling you I believe Jerome
is a snitch.

                    GARY
Ain't no way, I've known Jerome for
years, the guy is cool man!

                    BRYAN
Well, there's one way to find out.

                    GARY
What are you planning to do?

                    BRYAN
Let's set him up, - Let's talk about
something we're going to do in front
of him, and see if the cop's show up.

                    GARY
Okay, - man I hope you are wrong -
cause I will kill his ass!

The waiter is coming back with Mason Food

                    MASON
          I'm sorry, I Just notice the time, and
          I have to meet a friend. Could you put
          that in a box for me?

                    WAITER
          Sure, no problem.

The waiter leaves and returns with his food.

                    MASON
          Thank you.

Gives her a generous tip, moving quickly to his
car, locating Rico's number and call him.

                    RICO
          Rico speaking

                    MASON
          Hey Rico, do you have a minute?

                    RICO
          Who is this?

                    MASON
          This is Mason, The guy from Chicago,
          we met earlier today.

                    RICO
          Oh yeah, What's up?

                    MASON
          I stopped at this Restaurant to get a
          bite to eat. These two guys came in, I

over heard them talking about Jerome
being a snitch: and they are going to
set him up.

                    RICO
Did they say how they were going to
set him up?

                    MASON
Yeah, the one guy said, they were
going to talk about something they
were going to do in front of Jerome.
If the Police shows up, they will know
that Jerome snitched. Hey, this might
be my brother.

                    RICO
Laughs.

                    MASON
Why did you laugh?

                    RICO
I didn't mean to laugh, but you did say
he was your twin, right?

                    MASON
Yeah, but why did you laugh?

                    RICO
Well, the Jerome I Know looks nothing
like you. I just thought it was funny,
because he always make me laugh. But
tell me more!

                    MASON
I tried to tell you this earlier, we're
not identical, my Aunt Joyce said he
looks like his Dad.

                    RICO
Silence.

                    MASON
Hello - why are you quite, do you know
a Jerome that looks like his Dad?

                    RICO
Yes I do!

                    MASON
Rico, this could be my brother man -
but is he really a snitch?

                    RICO
I will explain everything to you later,
but right now I need to contact Jerome,
hang tight, I'll call you tomorrow, all
right!

                    MASON
Okay, please don't forget, I'll be
waiting to hear from you.

Rico calling Jerome...

                    JEROME JR.
Hey, what's up man?

> RICO

Hey Jerome, check this out, I need to
see you, are you helping out at the
shelter this evening.

Feeding the homeless is a part of Jerome community
service and a (S. O. I.) Instead of jail time.

> JEROME JR.

Yeah, That's where I'm at now, I'll be
free to talk around 8:30

> RICO

Okay, I'll see you then.

SAME DAY - WE NEED A SPY!

Bryan and Gary are still at the restaurant eating.

> BRYAN

You know Jerome works at the shelter
doing community service, instead of
jail time. That's one of the reasons
why, I don't trust him.

> GARY

So if he had did jail time instead of
community service he would be cool. Do
you see how stupid that sounds? Man,
Jerome is cool all right!

> BRYAN

Yeah, he's cool, but something ain't
right, I can feel it.

                         GARY

Well what are you going to do? I see
you are not going to let this go!

                         BRYAN

I'm just thinking, - Jerome don't know
Robert do he?

                         GARY

I don't know, well I'm not sure. But,
what are you thinking?

                         BRYAN

I'm going to ask Robert to go to the
shelter, and see if Jerome is talking
to anyone that looks out of place.
For all we know they might have under
cover cops working in the shelters.

                         GARY

Wow - okay - I hadn't thought about it
like that! All right - call him!

                         BRYAN

Ring ring

                         ROBERT

Hey, what's up Bryan.

                         BRYAN

I need you to do something for me. But
first, I need to know, have you ever
met Jerome?

                         ROBERT
Jerome, Jerome.

                    BRYAN
The guy we told you about that got
busted, the one doing community
service, instead of jail time.

                    ROBERT
Oh, yeah, yeah. I have seen him around.

                    BRYAN
But you have never met?

                    ROBERT
No I haven't! - What's up, and why all
the questions?

                    BRYAN
Personally I think Jerome is a snitch
or as they call it (S. O. I). I'm
asking you to go to the shelter, and
observe who he talks to.

                    ROBERT
No problem Brother, I'm on top of it.
I'll call you later.

SAME DAY, NIGHT- RICO MEET WITH JEROME

Rico dressed like a homeless guy meets with
Jerome. They sit at a table together. Rico looking
at Jerome, and having a picture of mason in his
mind, begin to laugh.

                    JEROME JR.
What's up - what are you laughing at?

                    RICO
I'll tell you later, but right now I
have to make sure you are safe.

                 JEROME JR.
Safe - (eyes moving swiftly from side
to side). Safe from what or who - what
are you talking about?

                    RICO
Listen, I don't have any answers right
now, you know how I give my card to
people. Well someone call me, and said
he heard two guys talking about setting
you up. Because they think you are a
snitch. So when you are approached be
smart. I really don't know what these
guys are up to, okay!

                 JEROME JR.
Okay, but who told you about these
guys?

                    RICO
I'll tell you when I get more information
on this person.

Rico, with his keen sense of the way people operate,
notice a guy standing in a corner watching them
talk.

                 RICO (CONT'D)
Don't look, there is a guy standing
in the corner to your right with a
gray jacket on. He has been staring
at us for about five minutes or more.

Go over, and say some kind words to him, and walk away. I want to see his response.

Jerome walks over to the Guy

                    JEROME JR.
Hey sir.

                    ROBERT
(Turns) Are you talking to me?

                    JEROME JR.
Yeah, did you get anything to eat?

                    ROBERT
No, but I'm all right!

                    JEROME JR.
Are you sure, because we have plenty of food!

                    ROBERT
No - I'm all right! I was just checking this place out, and I will be back.

                    JEROME JR.
Okay, we're here every Thursday and you are more than welcome.

                    ROBERT
Okay, and thank you, but I have to go.

Rico has already went out side waiting for the guy to come out. Then follows him to see who he is involved with. After about two blocks Robert thinks he's being followed. So he calls Bryan.

                    ROBERT (CONT'D)
Hey Byran, I'm on the Boulevard
approaching 4Th st. I think I'm being
followed. Meet me on 6Th & the Boulevard

Robert friends met him at 6St. and the Boulevard,
Rico see the other two guys meet him, and began
to cross the street.

                    ROBERT(CONT'D)
    Hey!!

RICO Keeps walking

                    ROBERT
    Hey, I'm talking to you!

                    RICO
    Why are you talking to me?

                    ROBERT
    You were at the shelter right?

Rico thinking that, because he saw him at the
shelter he might be cool, and not start anything.

                    RICO
    Smiles, yeah, and I saw you there, you
    were talking to what's his name, ah -
    Jerome, when I left.

They start to walk toward him.

                    ROBERT
    I ask you a question!

                    RICO
What??

                    ROBERT
Are following me?

                    RICO
Naw man, and why would I be following you?

                    BRYAN
Let's jack his ass up!

                    GARY
Come on guys, leave the man alone, you
see he don't have anything!

                    BRYAN
Looking at Roscoe, Well, sometime you
can be in the wrong place at the wrong
time. Began to walk toward Rico.

                    RICO
(Backing up,- pull out his gun. I
wouldn't try that if I were you. You
need to listen to your friend, and
leave this guy alone. I really don't
want any trouble.

                    GARY
Awe shit he got a gun, Dam it Bryan,
I told you to leave the man alone. (
Turns to Rico) Sir, I want you to see
I didn't have anything to do with this.

                    BRYAN
Dam Gary, you going to punk out like
that?

                    GARY
Man I'm not going to get shot over
something stupid, the man haven't did
anything to you.

                   ROSCOE
I don't believe any bullets in that
thing. (Staring at Rico).

                    GARY
Why in the hell would you even think
something like that?

                   ROSCOE
(Gets right in Rico's face,- stares him
in the eyes, then backs up with a smile
on his face). See, that's what I'm talking
about. Ain't no bullets in that gun. He
probably use that thing to rob people.

Now all of them are looking at Rico with anger.

                    GARY
I didn't think about that...

                   ROSCOE
You know, and I know, if there were
bullets in that gun he wouldn't be
letting me, - I'll rephrase that: I
wouldn't be taking this kind of crap, (
then he start prancing trying to look
tough). I would be bursting a cap in
you punks ass.

                    RICO
Shoots him in the ass, you mean like
that?

                    ROSCOE
He shot me in the ass.

                     RICO
Now I'm going to ask you guys again
to leave me alone; and no one else
will get hurt. You better get him to
a doctor.

                    ROSCOE
(Holding his butt and sobbing with
pain). That was probably the only bullet
he had in that gun.

                     RICO
You want me to shoot you in the ass
again?

They are staring at Rico as if it were his last
bullet, because they are mad now, because he shot
Roscoe. Rico fired another shot in the air.

                 RICO (CONT'D)
Now do anyone of you punks feel lucky -
That could have been my last bullet.
Now get him to a doctor before he bleed
to death.

Someone had call the police, reporting gun shots
in the area, and as they were patrolling they see
these guys. Bryan waves his hands.

                     BRYAN
Over here Officer, this guy shot my
friend.

The officer recognized Rico, and didn't want to
blow his cover. They made sure their guns were on
safety before he pointed it at Rico. Walks over
to Rico and pats him down and takes his gun,
handcuffed him, and walked him to the car.

                    RICO
      Man I'm so glad y'all showed up! I
      thought I was going to have to kill
      one of them fools.

                    OFFICER TIM
      What happen?

                    RICO
      Well, someone told me these guys, I
      don't know if it were these guys or
      not, but he said he heard two guys
      talking about Jerome. They think he
      is a snitch, and they were going to
      set him up to prove it. So I went to
      the shelter to let him know. While we
      were talking I notice this guy staring
      at us for about five minutes or more,
      So I told Jerome to go and show him
      some kindness, I just wanted to see
      his reactions.

                    OFFICER TIM
      Yeah, but why did you shoot him?

                    RICO
      (Laughing shaking his head from side to
      side), I have never seen anything like
      this in all my years on the force. The
      guy that I shot in the ass; I mean - I

showed him my gun. He looked at me, then came to the conclusion that I didn't have any bullets in my gun. I was too poor to effort them. One of his friends said man don't be stupid, and what make you think there's no bullets in that gun? For one look at him, and two, then he start prancing around, talking about if he had a gun with bullets in it, he wouldn't take no crap off of anybody. I'll be bursting a cap in all y'all asses, and I could tell from there actions they were listening to this fool, so I shot him in the ass!

OFFICER TIM
Man you know you could have...

RICO
Wait! It gets crazier, as he laid sobbing in pain, I could not believe what he said! (Starting to laugh again).

OFFICER TIM
Well, what did he say?

RICO
He said, that was probably the only bullet I had in the gun. I had to fire another shot in the air to convince them fools. It's crazy, anyway take me to my car, this has been a long, and crazy day.

OFFICER TIM
You know I have to make a report, right?

                         RICO
Yeah, but I am tired, I will do it in
the morning, but right now, I am going
home, and apologize to my wife.

                      OFFICER TIM
Apologize?

                         RICO
Yeah, well, I told her that I would be
home at 8 and it's 10, so yes!

Rico gets home around 10:30 his wife is waiting.

                      RICO (CONT'D)
I'm sorry babe, you wouldn't believe
this day!

                         LISA
Honey you have had bad days, so, -

                         RICO
Sweetie, not like this one, I think it
was more crazy than anything I have
experienced since I've been a cop.

                         LISA
Okay, what happen?

                         RICO
Telling her what happen, but he began
to demonstrate the whole scene to Lisa.

                         LISA
She laughing so hard, Honey it's not
funny that you shot someone, but who
could be so stupid?

                    (MORE)

                 LISA (CONT'D)
Especially when he said that's probably
the only bullet you had in the gun.

                   RICO
I'm not going to lie, when he said
that, I start to shoot him in the head
for being so stupid. Anyway will you
warm my food up again; while I shower?

                   LISA
Sure honey.

Kisses her, and leaves the room. After eating he
peaks in on his daughter, and she's still awake.

                   RICO
Hey sweetheart I thought you were a
sleep.

                 DAUGHTER
I was hoping you would come see me,
cause I'm not sleepy, and I want to
spend some time with you.

                   RICO
I'm sorry sweetheart, but daddy need to
spend some time with mama. (Kisses her
on the forehead) - I'm off Wednesday,
and we will have the whole day together.

                 DAUGHTER
Just you and I dad?

                    RICO
You don't want mama to come?

                  DAUGHTER
No dad, just you and I!

                    LISA
I heard that.

                  DAUGHTER
Put's her hands over her mouth, and
stares her dad in the eyes.

                    RICO
Kisses her on the forehead again, it
will be okay she understands. But I
will see you in the morning, (with a
big hug) good night.

Go's to be with Lisa, they make love.

                RICO (CONT'D)
Lying there staring at the sealing
shaking his head from side to side with
a smile on his face.

                    LISA
Honey is everything okay?

                    RICO
Yeah, - something else happen earlier
today. This guy said he just got here
this morning from Chicago. We had a
little run in, but he claimed he's
looking for his twin brother. He said
they were separated at a very young age.

                    LISA (CONT'D)
So what's the problem? I mean I...

                    RICO
Well, he said his mother died and he
found some papers stating he has a
twin brother. Now check this out, he
says his twin looks nothing like him.
He looks like his dad, and when he told
me has brothers name: it made me kind
of believe him.

                    LISA
What's his name?

                    RICO
Laughs, Jerome.

                    LISA
Our Jerome?

                    RICO
I don't know, but that boy looks just
like his dad. I going to get his last
name tomorrow, and do a check on him.
Jerome is our S.O.I., and we have gotten
pretty tight. So I have to protect
him. - Okay I have to get some sleep.

                    LISA
Okay, kiss, good night

NEXT DAY, MORNING: SNOOPY

                    DENNIS
Hey boss, I can't come in today.

SNOOPY
What's wrong, - is everything all right?

DENNIS
Yeah, yeah just not feeling to good!

SNOOPY
Yeah I heard old man Jerome whipped that ass real good yesterday. Is that the reason you're not feeling so good?

DENNIS
Who told you that?

SNOOPY
Nigger I know shit before it happens, now you bring your ass in or find another job. What did you do to piss him off?

DENNIS
I rather Not talk about that!

SNOOPY
Okay well I will see you within the hour, Bryan just walked in. What's up Bryan?

BRYAN
Bad news boss, - Roscoe is in the hospital, he should be getting out today, They kept him for observation.

SNOOPY
What happen?

                    BRYAN
This homeless guy shot him. Roscoe
didn't believe the guy had bullets in
his gun.

                    SNOOPY
Looking confused - you mean he saw
the gun, and came to that conclusion,
where did he shoot him at in the head?

                    BRYAN
He shot him in the ass, just missing
a main artery.

                    SNOOPY
But why would he be so stupid - when
someone shows you a gun, I mean what
made him think that?

                    BRYAN
I guest Roscoe thought the guy couldn't
afford bullets.

                    SNOOPY
He should've shot his ass in the head.
Did you get anything on Jerome?

                    BRYAN
No, but the guy that shot Roscoe was at
the shelter talking to Jerome. Robert
called Roscoe, Gray and I to meet him
on 6st. and the Boulevard, we were
going to Franks. Robert saw the guy
again, and asked him: are you following
me? Then Roscoe started talking trash,
and wined up getting shot in the ass.

SNOOPY
What happen to the guy?

BRYAN
The Police showed up think God, and arrested him.

SNOOPY
Wow, Dennis got his ass beat by a 80 year old man. I don't know if he's that old. But anyway, and Roscoe gets shot in the ass. I still don't know if Jerome is working for the cops.

BRYAN
That was our plan, to set him up, but he was talking to that guy that shot Roscoe in the ass.

SNOOPY
How were you going to set him up?

BRYAN
Talk about doing something in front of him. If the cops show up: Then we will know that he informed them.

SNOOPY
I like that idea, pursue that!

NO MORE HOMELESS GUY: SAME DAY MIDDAY.

RICO
(Talking to his supervisor): I have to change my look, because if them punks see me at the shelter it could be trouble for them, you know what I'm saying. So this is my new look!

                    TIM
You going to come to work looking like
that?

                    RICO
If I can come to work dressed like
a homeless person for the last five
years. Which almost caused me to kill
some one, So yes, I'm going to come to
work dressed like this until we have
solved this case, or maybe until I
retire.

                    TIM
Man we need you on this case, and you
can't go to the shelter looking like
that!

                    RICO
Who said I was going to the shelter!?
Have you ever heard of a night club
called Franks.

                    TIM
Yeah, but I have never been there, but
how will you keep in touch with Jerome?
We need to know what...

                    RICO
Hold tight - I'm going to talk to Frank
and see if He will let him work there,
and I was told that Snoopy hangs out
there.

MEETING WITH FRANK: LATER THAT EVENING.

RICO
Walking through the door.

HOSTESS
Welcome to Franks!

RICO
Thank you! Will you tell Frank Rico
is here.

HOSTESS
Is he expecting you?

RICO
Please, just tell him Rico is here!

HOSTESS
Mr. Frank, Rico is here to see you.

FRANK
Rico?! Tell him I will be right down.

HOSTESS
He will be right down.

RICO
Thank you!

FRANK
Rico, man it's been along time - and
look at you, man I like that hook up!
What brings you by?

RICO
I have a serious situation: I'm on a case
involving two homicides. A few night ago

I had to do something that might have
blown my cover as a homeless person.

> (MORE)

                RICO (CONT'D)
So this is my new image. My source of
information works at the shelter. I'm
asking you to give him a job here so
I can keep in touch with him - he's a
hard worker.

                FRANK
I will see what I can do!

                RICO
I was hoping you could do something
soon.

                FRANK
How soon?

                RICO
Frank this is a very serious case.
Would it be asking to much if I say
tomorrow night?

                FRANK
For you Rico, I will do it!

                RICO
Thank you! I promise you we will
just blend right in, and we will not
jeopardize your business in any way.
You are doing a great service to this
city. We don't need scum bags like that
on the streets.

                    FRANK
Who is this guy?

                    RICO
Come on Frank, you know I can't give
out that info. This is an undercover
job, but I heard he dines here a lot.

                    FRANK
You know you can trust me.

                    RICO
Okay, we will talk about that. But can
I call Jerome to tell him to come in
tomorrow night?

                    FRANK
Yeah, I could use a waiter or maybe a
dish washer.

                    RICO
I haven't talk to him yet, I had to
talk to you first hoping you would say
yes. I will call him now. (Ring, ring).

                    JEROME JR.
Rico, what's up my brother?

                    RICO
Hey - have you ever heard of Franks
night club?

                    JEROME JR.
Franks on alpine & 7th?

                    RICO
Yeah!

                    JEROME JR.
Man you need money to hang out there!

                    RICO
If I told you that I got you a job
there would you be interested?

                    JEROME JR.
Yeah! But doing what?

                    RICO
I don't know, he told me that he would
fine something for you.

                    JEROME JR.
Okay Rico - what is all this about?

                    RICO
I can't be seen at the shelter anymore.
Remember that guy that was standing
at the door, and I told you to go and
say something to him?

                    JEROME JR.
Yeah!

                    RICO
I had to shoot his friend in the ass
last night.

                    JEROME JR.
That was you?

                    RICO
Yeah, so I can't be seen at the shelter
anymore. So I'm changing my image from

a homeless guy to a successful business man. I got word that Snoopy and his entourage comes in for the last show.

JEROME JR.
I'm sorry bro. I could have told you that, I mean I was one of the little guys but I would hear them talking about Franks. Did you say you got me a job there?

RICO
Yeah, and you can start tomorrow night!

JEROME JR.
This might be my lucky break!

RICO
What do you mean by that?

JEROME JR.
You will see! I will talk to you latter. - (Calls Grady).

GRADY
(Ring, ring - Looking at his phone, Jerome - answers it), is this the one and only Jerome?

JEROME JR.
Man I was hoping you still had the same number. I was told you guys play at Frank's now.

GRADY
Yeah, what's up?

                    JEROME JR.
I can't tell you everything right now,
but a friend of mine got me a job at
Franks, he didn't tell me what I would
be doing. - but you know me!

                    GRADY
What do you have in mind?

                    JEROME JR.
I know it's been years, but do you still
do that song I use to opening with?

                    GRADY
Yeah, all we need to do is tighten it up.

                    JEROME JR.
I'm going to walk in at eight. When
you see me, just kick it; and I will
do my thing.

                    GRADY
Man - I'm excited about this, I'm going
to call Calvin, and let him know.

                    JEROME JR.
Okay, I will see you tomorrow night.

MASON MEETS HIS FAMILY: NIGHT

                    MASON
Ring, ring.

                    RICO
Mason, man I was going to call you.
What is your last name?

MASON

Peterson, why you ask?

RICO

I been thing about you and your twin, Jerome. His last name is Peterson.

MASON

Is it anyway I can meet him? I need to tell him, and dad about mom!

RICO

Yeah, what are you doing tonight?

MASON

I've been waiting to here from you, I don't know my way around hear yet.

RICO

Where are you staying?

MASON

The Royal Inn on main and six st. I stopped in a club last night called Franks. Man - they have good food, and a house band that's really good. The service was good so I might stop in there tonight.

RICO

Wow, I'm amazed at how all this is coming together, because I called you to invite you to Franks tonight. Jerome said he will be there by eight, I'll be there at 7:30. I will see if he will invite his Dad! Can you make it?

                    MASON
I can be there by 7:30!!

                    RICO
They have a 8 o clock and a 10 o clock
show, so That will be perfect, see you
then.

                    JEROME JR.
Calling his Dad.

                    JEROME SR.
(Ring ring) Hey Jr. What's up?

                    JEROME JR.
What are you doing tonight?

                    JEROME SR.
I'm going to take Louis over to Franks,
they have good food and a house band
that's really good.

                    JEROME JR.
Dad I called you to invite you to
Franks, my friend got me a job there.

                    JEROME SR.
Doing what?

                    JEROME JR.
I don't know what he has in mind, but
I talked to Grady, He's the leader of
the house band at Franks.

                    JEROME SR.
Son, - you going to do your thing?

                    JEROME JR.
You know I am dad!

                    JEROME SR.
Don't be surprised if your Dad join you.

They both laugh.

THE INFAMOUS DANCE BROUGHT THEM TOGETHER: NIGHT.

                    RICO
(Pulls up in a Mercedes - walking
toward the entrance.

                    OTIS
Keep it moving, keep it - well, well -
who you posing to be, Mr. Big Stuff?

                    RICO
Smiling - I'm here to see Frank.

                    OTIS
Is he expecting you?

                    RICO
Yes he is!

                    OTIS
Laughing, I'm just giving you a hard
time.

                    NO NAME
Yeah like you always do, - people are
going to get tired of you messing with
them, old man!

                    OTIS
Didn't I see you last week?

                    NO NAME
Yeah!

                    OTIS
Did you see the ass whipping I put on
that young punk for doing what you just
did: running off at the mouth?

                    NO NAME
Yeah, but I ain't that young punk -
I will put your old ass to sleep!
(Looking at his boys).

                    OTIS
When I beat on a little punk,- Otis
loves a little spunk!. (Turns to Rico)-
What's your name Sir?

                    RICO
Rico.

                    OTIS
Rico: don't go anywhere, make sure his
friend don't try to help him.

                    RICO
Okay, I can do that!

                    OTIS
I'm going to give you a chance to
apologize for running off at the mouth.

                    NO NAME
I ain't apologizing to your old ass!

                    OTIS
Rico you're my witness, I gave him a
chance to apologize right?

                    RICO
(Thinking to himself, this young man
is going to hurt this old guy) Yeah!

Otis gives him a round house kick to the head
knocking him out.

                    OTIS
I have gotten to old to be wrestling
with these young punks.

                    RICO
Man - that was pretty impressive!
Laughing, Can I go in now? (As he is
walking away, he hears Otis giving
someone else a hard time turns and
see mason).

                    OTIS
Well, well, well who is this dressed
in all white?

                    RICO
(Quickly runs back) Otis this is my
friend he's cool!

                    OTIS
Well get him out of my face, because
I don't like the way he looked at
me, swelling all up with an attitude,
because I touched his white suit. Boy
I will beat you out of that suit!!

                    MASON
Looking confused, man what is wrong
with you? I didn't look at you in a
certain way - and do I know you sir.?

                    RICO
Yes, come with me, and I will tell you.
As they are walking, I'm Rico.

                    MASON What?
Man you...

                    RICO
Hey - this is strictly undercover work.
You and the owner are the only one's,
and your twin are the only one's who
knows I'm a cop, So I can't blow my
cover. (Turns to the hostess) - Hello
again, will you tell my friend I'm hear?

                    HOSTESS
Sure will, Mr. Frank, Rico is here.

                    FRANK
Okay tell him I will be down in about
10 minutes.

                    HOSTESS
He will be down in about 10 minutes.

                    RICO
Okay, This is my friend Mason we
will sit at the bar, - and you look
marvelous!

                    MASON
I totally agree!!

                    HOSTESS
Oh, thank you guys!

                    FRANK
Rico my friend, where is ahh, what's
his name?

                    RICO
Jerome, He will be here around eight.
This is his brother visiting from
Chicago, (looking at Mason) can I
tell him?

                    MASON
Tell him what?

                    RICO
That this will be your first time
meeting.

                    MASON
You've already said it now!

                    FRANK
Really! This will be your first time
meeting, why is that?

                    MASON
I was very young when we were separated,
and I found out from reading some
papers I found under my mom bed.

                    FRANK
You're going to meet him tonight for
the first time?

                    MASON
Yeah, and I'm nervous, I really don't
know what to expect!

                    FRANK
You said he would be here by eight
right? (Looking at his watch), it's a
quarter to now.

                    RICO
(Remembering how Otis was giving people
a hard time), I'm going to go, and make
sure Mr. Otis don't hurt my man.

                    (MORE)

                    RICO (CONT'D)
(Go's out side) Otis I have one more
friend coming, he's going to be working
here so don't give him a hard time.

                    OTIS
What's his name?

                    RICO
Jerome Jr.

                    OTIS
Is he the son of Jerome the pimp?

                    RICO
Yeah!

                    OTIS
He comes in here all the time with
Louis. Old Otis would like to tap that.
But when he get's here I will let him
right in.

                    RICO
Thank you!

The eight o clock show starts and the band is kicking it. Then Jerome walks through the door.

                    JEROME JR.
Jerome's in the house I said Jerome's in the house, Breaks out into his infamous dance.

                    RICO
(Was getting ready to tell him to tone it down) Jerome!

                    FRANK
No - look at my customers, they're loving this guy.

                    MASON
(Watching) - Rico That's how I dance!

                    RICO
You can dance like That?

                    MASON
I can show you better than I can tell you. - Gets up, and starts to dance.

                    JEROME JR.
(Feeling a little threatened), tried to step it up.

                    MASON
Matched every move he made.

                    JEROME SR.
Who is this doing my dance? My son is the only one I taught that dance too.

But I have some moves that I haven't showed anyone. - Gets up and steals the show.

                    JEROME JR.
I don't know who you is, but where did you learn how to dance like that?

                    MASON
I was surprised to see you doing my dance. But I haven't never seen moves like dad's!

                    JEROME SR.
Boy,- where did you learn to dance like that?

                    MASON
I don't know! I have danced like this all my life, I guess it's in my jeans.

                    JEROME JR.
Negro you don't even have on jeans!!

                    MASON
Staring at the both of them - I'm your son, and you are my twin brother.

                    JEROME JR.
Burst out laughing, My twin brother I...

                    JEROME SR.
Wait a minute Jr., - let's go over here and talk.

                    MASON
When I tell you my mother's name, you
will know that I'm telling you the truth.

                  JEROME SR.
Well, I want to hear what you have
to say.

                    MASON
I'm so excited about meeting you. I
hate to spoil this with bad news. But
we buried our mom two weeks ago.

                  JEROME JR.
Dad what is he talking about?

                  JEROME SR.
I don't know, maybe if he give some
names it might make since.

                    MASON
(Pull out a picture of him and Sarah
back in the day). Do you remember her?

                  JEROME SR.
Sarah, - Sarah died?

                  JEROME JR.
Let me see that picture (looking at it)
this was my mother? Dad you never said
anything about her.

                  JEROME SR.
Son - please forgive me, but you
wouldn't understand the situation.

                    MASON
Dad just tell him the truth. - I'll
tell him, dad was a pimp, and he didn't
want to change. So mom wouldn't marry
him, and from what aunt Joyce told me.
He wanted to take us both but mom said
you can take only one so he took you.

                    JEROME JR.
I have had a brother these many years,
and didn't know it?

                    MASON
Come on bro. We are together now, so
let's make the best of it. We can't
change the past, but we can have a
beautiful future.

                    JEROME SR.
I like the way you think, and they
hugged.

                    RICO
That's what I was hoping to see. Want
to hear something funny?

                    FRANK
Yeah, what's so funny? (As he take a
sip of wine).

                    RICO
Mason is Jerome's twin brother.

                    FRANK
(Holding his mouth trying to keep from
spraying wine on Rico). Man don't do
that!

                    RICO
That's what He told me.

                    FRANK
That's hard to believe but, - Hang
tight. I see Snoopy and his gang are
here. - (Walking over to Snoopy),
Snoopy my man!! I have a surprise for
you tonight.

                    RICO
(Sees Roscoe coming in on crutches
turns and walks away over to where
Mason, Jerome and dad are).

                    SNOOPY
You know I don't like surprises!

                    FRANK
You're going to love this one, I will
send the girls over.

                    RICO
I must say, you guys were amazing!
Mason, when you told me that you dance
like that - I was thinking, I can't
believe Jerome is dancing like that
and you did it! Then dad joined in
and stole the show. Man that was truly
amazing.

                  JEROME JR.
You know him?

                    RICO
Yeah! Looking at Mason laughing.

                    MASON
It's funny now, but not so funny the
day we met. But I am so glad we met,
because I found my family because of
you, and I thank God!

                    RICO
Jerome you're going to do your stand
up at 10 right?

                    JEROME JR.
Yeah, and I need to talk to Grady.

                    RICO
Okay - (turning to Mason) that midget
over there is one of the most notorious
guys in the city.

                    MASON
Really? - The guy that's next to the one
on crutches was with someone else at
the other place talking about setting
Jerome up.

                    RICO
I can't talk about it now - but the
one on crutches, He's the one I shot
in the ass...

                    MASON
Laughing - what, did you say you shot
him in the ass?

                    RICO
I can't go in to details right now,
but they set your brother up, accusing

him of killing two people. Two years
in prison for something he didn't do.

                    MASON
So he is a snitch?

                    RICO
If that's what you want to call it -
but, it's more than that now - he's like
a little brother. This is something he
wanted to do!

                    JEROME JR.
Walking up to Grady giving him a high
five.

                    GRADY
Man who was that guy that was matching
every move you made?

                    JEROME JR.
It's a long story but, - I'm just finding
out that I have a brother.

                    GRADY
That's your brother?

                    JEROME JR.
Yeah, - we will talk about that later.
Frank want me to do the 10 o clock
show also.

                    FRANK
(Walking swiftly toward Jerome) Brother
are ready to turn it out?

                    JEROME JR.
Yes I am; just making sure Grady knows.

                    FRANK
I want to introduce you!

                    JEROME JR.
Well That settles that.

                    FRANK
You want to be introduced as Jerome or
do you prefer something else.

                    GRADY
He was called the wonder man!

                    FRANK
The wonder man?

                    GRADY
They were wondering how he was doing
those moves. That's why it blew me away
when I saw that other guy dancing like
Jerome...

                    FRANK
So, Jerome the wonder man is okay?

                    JEROME JR.
That will work for me!

                    FRANK
Okay, you disappear and I will call
you at 10

JEROME JR.
(On his way to the dressing room stops at the table where Mason and his dad is sitting) Hey bro. I'm going on at 10, don't steal my show!

MASON
I think you need to be worried about Dad stealing the show.

JEROME JR.
Yeah you're right, I will see you in a bit.

JEROME SR.
If you don't mind me asking, How did Sarah die?

MASON
They say it was a blood clot; all I know is she went to bed that night and didn't wake up that morning.

JEROME SR.
I'm so sorry son, but I am so glad you found us.

MASON
(Smiling nodding) - me too.

FRANK
Ladies and gentlemen we have a surprise guest tonight. They use to call him the wonder man, and he's with us tonight, come on put your hands together, and welcome Jerome the wonder man.

                    JEROME JR.
Jerome's in the house, I said Jerome's
in the house.

The ladies that knew him were screaming Jerome we
wondered what happen to you, Jerome we love you!

                    SNOOPY
Man I didn't know Jerome could dance
like - look at this dude.

When Jerome was done dancing, he did some stand
up comedy.

                    SNOOPY (CONT'D)
Bryan Go tell Jerome I want to see him.

                    BRYAN
(Walking over to Jerome) What's up
Jerome, Snoopy want to see you.

                    JEROME JR.
See me for what, the way you assholes
did me, - I don't have words for it.

                    BRYAN
Well he might be trying to make up for
what happen.

                    JEROME JR.
I know what happen - okay tell him I'll
be over in a few minutes. (Go's over
to Frank) can Rico and I meet in your
office?

                    FRANK
Meet in my office, for what?

                    JEROME JR.
Maybe Rico can fill you in, but this
is serious!

                      FRANK
I can tell,: Okay follow me, (Talking
to his Hostess). Go, and tell Rico to
meet me in my office.

She go's and tell Rico and he go's to Franks
Office.

                    JEROME JR.
I don't know what this is all about,
but snoopy wants to talk to me, and I
want to know what should I do.

                       RICO
If he offers you a job take it, - that
would put us right in the mist.

                    JEROME JR.
But that would put me -

                       RICO
You just have to be careful and smart. -
If he want you to work for him again,
don't take it right now. Make him think
you feel like he mistreated you, and
you don't want to have anything to do
with him, and his gang.

                    JEROME JR.
Okay - I just have to get myself
together mentally, because I want to
put my foot up his little ass!

                    RICO
I agree, I mean: getting yourself
together mentally. We can't blow it
now, this is the closes we have ever
been to solving this case.

                  JEROME JR.
Okay.

As Jerome is walking toward Snoopy's: these ladies
are talking among themselves.

                   COOKIE
Girl look at him with his fine ass,
watch this - (stands up looking the
other way, walks into him). I'm sorry!

                  JEROME JR.
Staring her in the eyes, (with a
whisper) Jerome's in the house - I said
Jerome's in the house!

Cookie gets weak in the knees and began to
stagger, Jerome catches her and helps her to her
seat.

              JEROME JR. (CONT'D)
Are you okay sweetheart?

                   COOKIE
Staring in his eyes: it's you, its
you! Oh my god - I'm so embarrassed. I
walked into you on purpose. I have had
a crush on you for years, and - then
you disappeared.

(MORE)

COOKIE (CONT'D)
Then I found out you were in prison, I was so heartbroken,- and no one would tell me anything!

JEROME JR.
Don't you go anywhere I want to talk to you: but I need to talk to this guy, it won't take long.

KATHY
Hey who is that guy that was dancing with you?

JEROME JR.
He's my brother, and believe it or not - (looking over at him) tonight is our first time meeting.

KATHY
Really!! Invite him over I'd like to meet him.

JEROME JR.
Hey mason, come meet these beauties.

MASON
(Comes over) Hello ladies.

JEROME JR.
Mason this is Cookie, and her friend Kathy. I don't mean to put you on the spot, but will you set with them? I have to go talk to someone. Leans over and kiss Cookie on the cheek I'll be back in a few.

                    COOKIE
          I'll be right here!

Jerome walking over to Snoopy's table.

                 COOKIE (CONT'D)
          (Talking to her girl friend) He is the
          most sexist man I have ever met!!!-
          Mason, Jerome told me that today is
          your first time meeting.

Mason tells the girls as much as he knows about
his new family.

SAME NIGHT: LET ME MAKE IT UP TO YOU.

                  JEROME JR.
          What's up Snoopy, Bryan told me you
          wanted to talk to me.

                   SNOOPY
          Man!!- I didn't know you had that kind
          of talent, that was very impressive.

                  JEROME JR.
          Yeah, - and if I hadn't lose two years
          of my life behind bars for something I
          didn't do - I could have been...

                   SNOOPY
          Brother after seeing what I saw
          tonight, - I know you would be a star
          in demand. If you let me make it up to
          you; - you know I can make it happen.
          Just come back and work for me, I need
          a man with your influence!

JEROME JR.
Come back and work for you? - Hell no,
I can't trust you Snoopy. I'm still on
probation thanks to you!

SNOOPY
Jerome I feel terrible about what
happen, but please let me make it up
to you. You know I have the Judges in
my back pocket. If you know what I
mean. - I can get you off probation as
soon as tomorrow! It won't be like it
was in the past, you will be one of
my top man!

JEROME JR.
I have seen how you treat your top guy.
They make a lot of money but they are
under your control. But you ought to
get me off probation anyway! Because
you know I didn't have anything to do
with those killings. - But if you get
me off probation I will give it some
serious thought.

SNOOPY
I will do that tomorrow, can I get a
phone number?

JEROME JR.
No! - Frank has given me a job and I
will be hear every weekend, and we can
communicate then. But I'm not giving
you my number. I will let you know next
week. - I have someone waiting on me.

                    SNOOPY
Who, Cookie?

                    JEROME JR.
- How do you know her?

                    SNOOPY
Shes my niece!

                    JEROME JR.
Really? (Backing away smiling) we will
be talking. (Thinking to himself, now
what I'm I going to do)?

Walking toward Cookie, she has this look on her
face.

                    COOKIE
Why are you talking to that asshole?

                    JEROME JR.
Wait a minute: he just told me that
you're his niece.

                    COOKIE
You really don't remember me ha? He
calls me his niece! My mom and dad
were killed and they worked for him.

                    JEROME JR.
I'm, - I'm sorry you lost your parents!

                    COOKIE
I can't prove it, but I believe snoopy
had something to do with it.

JEROME JR.
That was your parents? That's how I lost two year of my life, and I can't prove it - but I know Snoopy told Bryan and Roscoe to do something. I remember them coming by getting me, and the next thing I know, I woke up with the Police breaking through the door finding me with a gun in my hand. They were your parent's?

COOKIE
Yes, I some times fear for my life, because of what I know. I'm going to tell you now they are watching me. But I've been wanting to meet you for the longest time, and I see we have something in common.

JEROME JR.
Something in common - like what?

COOKIE
The both of us want to see him get what he deserves

JEROME JR.
Can I get a number or something so we can talk?

COOKIE
Yes: but I want to say this before I go. I have over heard them talking about you, and now it all make since, and yes they think you are a snitch. 'Wow' - they are watching me now.

I'm going to leave my business card with the hostess on the way out. Don't forget, and call me tonight. Mason it's so nice meeting you, but I have to go take care of some business. Kathy are you okay?

                    KATHY
Yes! I'm loving him - he was telling me about the day he came in town, Girl it's so funny. Okay call me in the morning.

                    COOKIE
Okay. (Looks at Jerome and kiss him on his cheek) don't forget to call.

                    JEROME JR.
Okay, (Watching her as she leaves) em my goodness! (Pull out his phone).

                    RICO
(Ring, ring) Jerome what's up?

                    JEROME JR.
Where are you?

                    RICO
I'm still up stars talking to Frank.

                    FRANK
Is That Jerome?

                    RICO
Yes.

                    FRANK
Tell him to come up so we can talk.

                    RICO
Come up, Frank want to talk to you
about working.

                    JEROME JR.
I'm on my way.

He stops by the hostess and gets Cookie's business
card, then go up stars.

                    JEROME JR. (CONT'D)
(Showing him Cookies card) I thank we
hit the jack pot tonight!

                    RICO
Okay fill me in!

                    JEROME JR.
Snoopy wanted to talk to me, as I was
walking toward him, this fine thing
came out of no where, her name is
Cookie.

                    FRANK
'Cookie' yes! She is a beautiful young
lady. I hate what happen to her parents.

                    RICO
What happen to her parents?

                    JEROME JR.
Her parent's are the ones I was framed
for killing. - This bastard had this

girls parents killed, then he adopts her as his niece. I got her number, - these are her exact words "I want to see his ass go down."

                    FRANK
You know Snoopy spends a lot of money here. But if he did something like that, I will do whatever I can, to help you bring him down - I can't believe what I'm hearing!!

                    RICO
What did you and Snoopy talk about?

                    JEROME JR.
He didn't know I had that kind of talent, and he need somebody like me with influence. Let me talk to Cookie first, I'm sure she knows something we don't know. I will call you later.

                    FRANK
That little bastard - I can't look at him the same any more.

                    RICO
Just do what you've been doing, we don't want to make him suspicious. I will see you tomorrow night.

                    FRANK
Okay man - be safe.

                    JEROME JR.
(Dialing Cookies number).

                    COOKIE
(Ring, ring) Hello.

                    JEROME JR.
Jerome's in the car, I'm just leaving
frank's, you want to meet somewhere?

                    COOKIE
Can you come by my place?

                    JEROME JR.
Yes, where do you live?

                    COOKIE
I can see Franks place from my window,
blank your lights.

                    JEROME JR.
Blank my light? Okay.

                    COOKIE
Yeah, I see you, you see the high rise
apartments to your left, I'm going to
blank my lights.

                    JEROME JR.
I see, what floor is that?

                    COOKIE
I'm on the 15th floor, I'll be waiting.

                    JEROME JR.
Okay I'll be right there!!

He Go's to her place, she let him in.

JEROME JR. (CONT'D)
(He comes in dancing: Jerome's in the
house, - 'Wow' this is nice!

COOKIE
(laughing) you're so funny. - Thank
you! But after seeing that fire; where
people were jumping out of windows. I'm
seriously thinking about moving.

JEROME JR.
I can understand that, but I like being
up high. (Staring her in the eyes). - I
need to know if I can trust you!

COOKIE
Are you serious?

JEROME JR.
Yes I'm serious, I know how that bastard
operates. Is he paying your rent?

COOKIE
Hell no, He offered though. - I guess
you didn't notice that I'm a realtor,
and doing very well. But why did you
ask if he was paying my rent?

JEROME JR.
Because that's one of the ways he
operates. Like Bryan, and Roscoe, he
have them by the balls. Because if
they don't do what he ask: they could
lose everything, nice cars and homes.
I can't prove it but I know in my heart
that one of them killed your parents,

and I'm leaning toward Roscoe. He's a heartless bastard!

                    COOKIE
(Staring him in the eyes) - you can trust me! (Walks closer) would you like something to drink, I have pinot noir and beer.

                    JEROME JR.
I'll have a glass of wine. - I hope my brother and Kathy like each other.

                    COOKIE
It looks like they were really having a good time and she said she was loving him!

SCENE CHANGE TO MASON AND KATHY: SAME NIGHT.

                    KATHY
Laughing, looking around we're the only two here.

                    MASON
I have to cash out.

                    KATHY
We don't have to leave, the place don't close until 1 and it's 12:30, I guess it is time to go.

                    MASON
We can stay for one more rdrink. Then I will go to my room, and watch some TV until I fall asleep.

                    KATHY
Where are you staying?

                    MASON
The Royal Inn on main & 6 st.

                    KATHY
I live in those condos right a cross the
street, and you are more than welcome
to come and have a drink with me there.

                    MASON
Well let's get out of here!

SCENE TO JEROME AND COOKIE: SAME NIGHT.

After a few glasses of wine they began to fill a
little tipsy

                    JEROME JR.
I'm feeling a little tipsy! When I feel
like this; all I want to do is make
love. So I think I better leave.

                    COOKIE
You don't have leave - But we can't
have sex. But I would love for you to
hold me. Let me sleep in your arms.

                    JEROME JR.
I did a lot of sweating tonight so I
need to shower.

                    COOKIE
Go shower, everything you need is in
the bathroom!

                    JEROME JR.
Comes out of the bathroom with a towel
rapped around him, dancing. Do you
have something I can put on?

                    COOKIE
(Trying to dance like him and laughing)
I have never seen any body move like
that. (She moves closer to him moving
her hips).

                    JEROME JR.
We better stop, it's been a while
for me.

                    COOKIE
You might not believe it: but I haven't
had sex in almost year now. About this
time last year, I accepted Jesus as
my savior. I want to do it right this
time.

                    JEROME JR.
This was meant to be, I accepted Him
while I was in prison.

                    COOKIE
Squeezing him real tight making a
groaning noise. Looks up at him -
do you think you could fall in love
with me?

                    JEROME JR.
Why would you ask a question like that?

                    COOKIE
Because, now that you're in my life, -
and I know I can fall in love with you.
I Know that sounds crazy! But you have
to understand that I've been into you
for a long time.

                  JEROME JR.
Jerome's in house.

                    COOKIE
Laughing you're so funny, - and I love
that about you, and the way you came
in last night, I mean everybody was
filling it and when your brother and
dad joined you: it was amazing, you
heard how the crowned was applauding!

                  JEROME JR.
To answer your question: let's just
take it slow and see where it goes,

- Jerome have had one to many heart breaks, but
I'm willing.

                    COOKIE
Kissing him - Jerome you don't ever
have to worry about that, I'm all yours
for as long as you want me, and I hope
you don't break my heart!!

                  JEROME JR.
And I am yours for as long as you want
me. Now we need to come up with a plan
to take Snoopy down.

                    COOKIE
Are you hungry?

                    JEROME JR.
Yeah, but I want to cook breakfast for
you, - hey you want to invite Kathy
and mason over?

                    COOKIE
'Yea' I would love that!

                    JEROME JR.
Dam, I don't have his number.

                    COOKIE
I have Kathy's number, maybe they are
together: I'll call her.

                    KATHY
Ring ring - Girl I was getting ready to
call you. I'm not going to lie, but I
almost slipped last night. But I slept
in his arms all night, and he was okay
with it because he's a christian.

                    COOKIE
Girl we had the same experience, I slept
in his arms all night, and we didn't
have sex. He got saved while in prison.

                    JEROME JR.
Jerome is in the house.

                    COOKIE
Laughing, stop it Jerome. The reason I
call: Jerome wants to invite you and
Mason over for breakfast.

KATHY

Mason was trying to show me how to do it, I have never seen them kind of moves, (laughing) but would you mind coming over here?

COOKIE

Honey, would you mind going over there?

JEROME JR.

No, I just want to spend sometime with my brother.

COOKIE

We will be over in about 20 minutes or so.

KATHY

Okay, we can let them bond and we can just - talk (laughing) See you in a bit! Mason your Brother and Cookie is on their way over, I invited them over to have breakfast with us.

MASON

(Pulls her lose to him) That was so thoughtful of you, because I do want to get to know him. So think you, - I really like you!

KATHY

(Putting her arms around his neck), and I really like you! (Kissing him) we better stop: we have company coming.

MASON

Okay, you go get dressed, I'm just going to throw on a T-shirt and I hope you don't mind me wearing your sweat pants.

KATHY

No, I was just thinking how sexy you look in them. Just make sure your T-shirt hide him. Not that she would, but I don't want any body getting any ideas. (Bending over talking to his penis) because you are mine now, you'll just have to wait. (BUZZ)

KATHY (CONT'D)

That must be them.

MASON

I'll let them in, go get dress.(Mason let them in and the music is playing). Mason opens the door.

JEROME JR.

Jerome's in the house - and began to dance.

MASON

(Laughing) joins him

KATHY

Cookie where are you? Girl you got to see this.

Cookie come running out: her and Kathy try to do the dance.

                    COOKIE
No wonder they call him the wonder
man. I've been trying to do those
moves, - it' unbelievable.

                    MASON
Embracing each other, is that how you
make your entrance where ever you go?

                    JEROME JR.
Pretty must!

                    MASON
Man I was so blown away when I saw you
dancing.

                    JEROME JR.
I was blown away when I saw you, and
how did you learn how to do our dance.

                    MASON
Brother! I

                    JEROME JR.
'Wow' you call me brother, you're the
brother I didn't know I had.

They both get teary-eyed and embrace again: and
the girls see them from the other room and they get
teary-eyed and go put their arms around them both.

                    MASON
I have all ways dance like that, I have
trophies for when I was in a dance
contest.

JEROME JR.
Me too, but it was when I was in
prison, - they had a night when everyone
would showcase their talent, it was a
lot of fun. But being in prison for
something you didn't do: takes the fun
out of everything.

MASON
Yeah tell me about it!

JEROME JR.
You saw the guy I was talking to last
night?

MASON
Talking about that midget?

JEROME JR.
That midget had her parent's kill and
I believe Bryan or Roscoe did it.

MASON
Killed who parent's?

JEROME JR.
Cookie's parent's and they set me up,
and made it look like I did it. I found
out from Snoopy: that the judge is
working for him too. But we are getting
ready to take him down!

MASON
What do you have in mind?

                    JEROME JR.
When I was in prison - Donald Jones is
his name. Cookie, sweetheart are you
computer savvy?

                    COOKIE
Yeah, what do you need to know?

                    JEROME JR.
See if you can find this guy on face
book.

                    COOKIE
If he is on Face Book we can talk to
him right now if he picks up.

                    JEROME JR.
Well look him up: he would be the
perfect guy to pull this off. He already
know what they did to me, and I know
he will help me.

                    COOKIE
Okay - types in his name.

                    JEROME JR.
What the hell, that's about a hundred
Donald Jones's.

                    COOKIE
They all have pictures next to their
names, we will look at them all and
hopefully he's in the mix. (Strolling
down)

                    JEROME JR.
Wait wait, back up - That's him!

COOKIE
Are you sure?

JEROME JR.
I'm positive! don't he look like a real
gangster? Call him.

DONALD
Ring ring, Who do I have the pleasure
of speaking to?

JEROME JR.
Is this Donald Jones?

DONALD
Yes it is, and who are you?

JEROME JR.
(Laughing) This is Jerome.

DONALD
'Jerome' Man I was thinking about you
the other day; how are you doing?

JEROME JR.
I'm doing good, and you?

DONALD
Man I'm riding high; I just opened my
store. You saw some of my designs, and
that man bag is selling like crazy;
I have ten people waiting for their
initialized bag. But enough about me,
what's going on.?

                    JEROME JR.
Do you remember me telling you about
Snoopy?

                    DONALD
Yeah, that's exactly what I was thinking,
when I thought about you.

                    JEROME JR.
I have a chance to take his ass down;
but I need some one with your looks to
pull this off.

                    DONALD
What do I have to do?

                    JEROME JR.
I should tell you this first, I'm
working with the Police. Do you have a
problem that?

                    DONALD
No I don't; what do you want me to do?

                    JEROME JR.
I just need you to pose as a big time
drug dealer.

                    DONALD
Oh hell yeah, you know I can pull
that off!

                    JEROME JR.
I will fill you in on everything, I
just needed to know if you would help
me. - So let me get everything in
place; and I will get back with you.

                    DONALD
I will be waiting to hear from you!

                   JEROME JR.
Okay (hanging up) 'Yes' - he's going
to help us?

                    COOKIE
But what are you planning to do?

                   JEROME JR.
Wait til you see this guy; I'm going
to have him pose as a big time drug
dealer. Snoopy keep asking me to come
work for him again; talking about how
much influence I have. So the next
time he ask, I'm going to accept his
offer. I have to call Rico and let him
know my plans.

DONALD COMES TO TOWN: ONE WEEK LATER.

Franks place has been booming since Jerome been
performing there: and snoopy keep asking him to
come work for him.

                    SNOOPY
 'Hey Jerome'

                   JEROME JR.
What do you want Snoopy?

                    SNOOPY
I did what I said, you're no longer on
probation.

                    JEROME JR.
So - you're going to hold that over my
head?

                    SNOOPY
No no, I'm just letting you know!

                    JEROME JR.
Well, show me some papers; and I will
let you know when I feel I can trust you.

                    SNOOPY
Here's the paper's, - come on man, what
do you have to lose?

                    JEROME JR.
Messing with someone like you? - I have
already lose two years of my life. So
I don't know: Maybe life.

                    (MORE)

                    JEROME JR. (CONT'D)
(Sarcastically talking about Snoopy
getting life in prison). I will let you
know tomorrow night.

                    SNOOPY
- I know we can make a lot of money
together, but if you can't give me an
answer right now, the deal is off!
Meaning you will be back on probation
as soon as tomorrow.

                    JEROME JR.
(Staring at him) - You said the pay is
good right?

SNOOPY
Yeah!

JEROME JR.
And I don't have to kill any body?

SNOOPY
What kind of monster do you think
I I'm?

JEROME JR.
Just staring at him.

SNOOPY
Okay, I just want to attract the
money. - I see the kind of people you
be talking too.

JEROME JR.
If I had known we were going to have
this conversation, - I mean: I could
have sole some tonight.

SNOOPY
That's what I'm talking Jerome! You
just have that swag, and we can be
making crazy money.

JEROME JR.
I can't say this guy is a friend, but
I know him pretty good. He lives in
Florida, and he would always have some
good coke. Now that I'm no longer on
probation I can take him a sample.
When he see how good your stuff is: we
will be in the money!!

                    SNOOPY
That sound like a plan.

                    JEROME JR.
I'll call him tomorrow, But Frank want
to see me. I'm going to see what he
wants, then I'm out of here.

                    SNOOPY
How are you and my niece doing?

                    JEROME JR.
Now that ain't none of your dam
business, and walks away.

                    DENNIS
(Trying to warm up to Snoopy) I didn't
like the way he disrespected you boss.
I will ...

                    SNOOPY
(Looking at him with a frown) - Didn't
his 80 year old dad, just beat that
ass about a month ago? You don't even
look taught anymore. Got your ass beat
by an 80 year old man.

                    DENNIS
He ain't that old!

                    SNOOPY
You probably thought that because of
the way he was whipping that ass. I
know he's not that old, but - Jerome is
going to make us a lot of money.

Jerome go's up stares.

                    JEROME JR.
     Frank - Rico left?

                    FRANK
     No, he's in the john.

                    RICO
     (Comes out) Jerome tell me something
     good.

                    JEROME JR.
     We got his ass! I was going to call you
     yesterday, but I got distracted. When
     I was in prison a guy name Donald and
     I became good friends. He now own's
     a clothing store in Florida. He knows
     what Snoopy and his boys did to me, and
     he's willing to help us bring him down.

                    RICO
     What is he going to do?

                    JEROME JR.
     - I got ahead of myself, - I accepted
     Snoopy's offer. He was telling me: I
     see the kind of people be coming up to
     you, and if I would come work for him
     again we can make a lot of money. I
     turned him down at first, but he gave
     me an ultimatum, he said if I didn't
     accept his offer tonight the deal is
     off; and I would be back on Probation
     as soon as tomorrow.

                    RICO
This is the first I've heard about a
deal.

                  JEROME JR.
I thought I told you, - The other night
when I told you he ask me to come work
for him again: you even told me don't
accept it right a way! Then I told
you - maybe I didn't tell you. But now
I know how Bryan, and Roscoe got away
with murder.

                    RICO
What did you find out?

                  JEROME JR.
When he was asking me to come back, I
told him I didn't want to take a chance
because I'm still on probation. He said
I have the Judge in my pocket.

                    RICO
Really, - he said he have the judge in
his pocket? - Man you're talking about
'Gerald'?

                  JEROME JR.
He was the one that prosecuted me - and
he said I can have you off probation
as soon as tomorrow, and he told me
today that It's done. So I guess I'm off
Probation. (Giving him a high five).

                    RICO
Good job, - but I can't believe that
Gerald would be so stupid! Anyway, tell
me about this guy - what is his name!

                  JEROME JR.
Donald.

                    RICO
Yeah, and what roll is he going to play
in all this?

                  JEROME JR.
Donald is going to pose as a big time
drug dealer from Florida. We give
Donald the money to buy the stuff,
and he brings the stuff to us. Then in
about two weeks, Donald is going to
tell him the stuff is selling so fast
he can't keep up with the demand, and
that he need to buy a large amount.
Then we will get him.

                    RICO
Boy I think you miss your calling,
that's a brilliant idea.

                  JEROME JR.
I'll call him right now.

                   DONALD
Ring, ring Hello.

                  JEROME JR.
Hey brother, it's Jerome: The stage is
set! When can you come up?

                    DONALD
I can be there Friday, is that okay?

                    JEROME JR.
Friday will be perfect. I will get you
a room at the Royal Inn. Then we will
go over the plot

                    DONALD
Sounds good, I will see you Friday.

                    JEROME JR.
Okay. (Hangs up) It's set - I will call
that midget tomorrow, and let him know
my man will be in town Friday, ready
to do business. But right now I have
to catch up with my girl. (Ring ring)
It's her - hey sweetheart.

                    COOKIE
Hi, where are you?

                    JEROME JR.
I'm still at Franks, I was just getting
ready to call you.

                    COOKIE
Yeah right!

                    JEROME JR.
Hey - Jerome don't lie - I have good
news, I'll see you in about ten minutes.

                    COOKIE
Okay, and I'm sorry for saying yeah
right: I just love you so much and I
want you here next to me!

                    JEROME JR.
I love you too, - let me talk to Frank
and Rico for a minute and I will be
there, (singing) just call Jerome and
he'll be there.

                    COOKIE
Laughing, I'll be waiting for you to
get here.

                    JEROME JR.
Okay bye (turning looking at Rico and
Frank) laughing.

                    RICO
Did I hear you say I love you too.

                    JEROME JR.
Yeah man: - wow, she has Jerome's heart,
but Jerome has her heart too. See you
guys Friday.

FRIDAY NIGHT AFTER THE SHOW: SNOOPY MEETS DONALD

Jerome and Donald are walking toward Snoopy.

                    DONALD
Snoopy is the midget Right?

                    JEROME JR.
Yeah - and I can't wait for his ass to
get what's coming to him!

                    SNOOPY
That must be the guy Jerome was telling
us about. (When they get closer)
Jerome my man; is this your friend
from Florida?

                    JEROME JR.
Yeah, Donald is his Name.

                    DONALD
Jerome told me you have the best!

                    SNOOPY
He told you right: I have the best and
I brought you a sample That you can
take with you.

                    DONALD
A sample, you...

                    SNOOPY
My shipment comes in tomorrow, and I
know you will be calling me. How much
do you want?

                    DONALD
I Have a select group of people that
I deal with, I'm talking 'big' money;
and Jerome is the only reason I'm
considering doing business with you.

                    SNOOPY
Looks at Jerome - nodding his head
with a smile.

                    DONALD
Jerome knows the quality of my stuff.
So I'm going on his word. But I flew
in today, and I'm flying out tomorrow.
I mainly wanted to see who I will be
doing business with.

SNOOPY

Can I buy you a drink or what ever you want.

DONALD

Thanks for the offer: but I'm going over to Jerome's place and we are going to do some lines and if it's as good as what I've been getting you will hear from me, but through Jerome.

SNOOPY

I don't have a problem with that, I'm just glad to have him on my team again. I know you will be calling because I have the best.

DONALD

That's what Jerome said, but tonight I will know for myself and If I like it, - well: I don't like talking on the phone, but I will let Jerome know how much I want. And I will be back Friday to do business.

SNOOPY

Sounds good - I know you're going to like it so I will see you Friday, and it's a pleasure meeting you.

DONALD

Thank you and it's a pleasure meeting you guy's.

As they are walking away.

                    SNOOPY
What do you guys think about Donald?

                    BRYAN
He seems cool to me, what about you
Roscoe?

                    ROSCOE
I like him, you can tell he been doing
this along time, I think we're getting
ready to blow up!

Jerome and Donald are trying to keep their cool
until they get out side, they get in the car and
burst off laughing.

                    JEROME JR.
Man you are good!

                    DONALD
(Still laughing) Man I was scared as
hell! - I ain't never seem someone that
small with that kind of power.

                    JEROME JR.
Man that bastard have some powerful
people in his web, crooked cops the
Judge! But all you have to do is show
your face one more time: which will be
Friday and after that I will tell him
that you are sending one of your man
to pick it up.

Which will be an undercover cop working with us.

DONALD
Okay: you have thought this thing
through!

JEROME JR.
All the way to the end - But I have
to get Bryan and Roscoe to confess to
killing my girls parent's. - Oh, I have
to call Rico.

RICO
(Ring ring) Jerome what's up?

JEROME JR.
Hey bro. Can you meet me at cookie's
place? We're leaving Franks now.

RICO
Yeah - I guess you can tell I'm eating,
but I will be there within the hour.

JEROME JR.
Okay see you there. Donald, do you need
anything from the store before we...

DONALD
I'm good man, but I didn't think I
would be feeling like this.

JEROME JR.
I'm sorry man: but you are the only
one, other than Rico and Cookie, knows
what that bastard did to me.

>   DONALD
> No no: I loved it, the adrenaline rush,
> and to be part of taking down the bad
> guy is something I will never forget.

BACK AT COOKIES PLACE: HE CAN'T HELP HIMSELF!

Buzz

>   COOKIE
> That's Jerome: now you know he's going
> to dance for about five minutes, so
> you might as well get ready to dance.

>   MASON
> Laughing so hard.

>   COOKIE
> Why are you laughing?

>   MASON
> I'll wait until we are done dancing and
> I will tell you all a very funny story.

Then Jerome comes in: ah, ah Jerome's in the
house. Cookie is getting pretty good at it. Mason
is laughing so hard he can't even dance!

>   COOKIE
> Kathy look - I'm getting it girl.

>   KATHY
> I see you! - Mason what is wrong with
> you - what are you laughing at?

Cookie stops the music: Jerome has one foot in
the air.

                    JEROME JR.
Hay who turned off the music? As you
can see I didn't finish my move.

                     COOKIE
Honey do you really want me to turn
the music back on, so you can put your
foot down?

                    JEROME JR.
Staring at the ceiling

                     COOKIE
Oh my God!

She turns the music back on so Jerome can finishes
his moves and Mason is laughing so hard he's in
tears.

                 COOKIE (CONT'D)
Your brother has a funny story to
tell us.

                     MASON
Wiping the tears from his eyes and
face, Brother all the way through
school, I got my butt whipped so many
times for dancing, but they couldn't
break me. I would come in the classroom
not saying word but doing our dance,
and the last time she sent me to the
Principle's office: I went in dancing,
all he could do was laugh. Then he
said: boy something is wrong with you!

They all are laughing. Buzz

                    JEROME JR.
          That must be Rico.

Rico comes in and they all sit down to talk.

                    JEROME JR. (CONT'D)
          Donald and I met with Snoopy and he
          thinks Donald is a big time drug
          dealer. Snoopy is going to be selling
          the stuff to me, thinking he's selling
          it to Donald.

                    (MORE)

                    JEROME JR. (CONT'D)
          Donald is going to show his face one
          more time when he comes back Friday.
          When we meet with Snoopy we will take
          an undercover cop; posing to work for
          Donald.

                    RICO
          I can do that!

                    JEROME JR.
          What if Roscoe recognize you?

                    RICO
          Man you know how good Paul is, you
          won't even recognize me.

JEROME MANIA: THE WONDER DANCE.

People are coming to Frank's from near and far
to see the wonder dance and taking it back to
their cities.

                    COOKIE
(Get's up to make coffee, turns the TV
on to watch the TODAY show and they
are talking about Jerome the wonder
man). Honey, honey wake up you want to
see this.

                    JEROME JR.
What!!!!

                    COOKIE
Your not going to believe this - quickly
calls Kathy.

                    KATHY
(Ring, ring) hey girl what up?

                    COOKIE
Turn on the TODAY show right now, and
I will talk to you later.

                    KATHY
Turns on the TV and hear them talking
about the wonder dance. Mason wake up,
I can't believe what I'm seeing.

They are showing people in different cities and
states even in China; trying to do the wonder
dance.

                    MASON
I can't believe what I'm seeing, -
'what'! I have to call Jerome.

                    KATHY
He's watching it, Cookie called me.

                    JEROME JR.
(Grab's Cookie and kiss her) Baby do
you know what this means.

                    COOKIE
Yeah, - you might get to big for me.

                    JEROME JR.
Do you remember what we said to each
other?

                    COOKIE
Yeah, but...

                    JEROME JR.
But nothing: what did we say to each
other.

                    COOKIE
I said; I would be with you as long as
you want to be with me.

                    JEROME JR.
...and what did I say?

                    COOKIE
You said the same thing.

                    JEROME JR.
Look at me, - read my lips: you are
stuck with me.

                    COOKIE
(With tears in her eyes she holds him
tight). I'm sorry honey, I've had some
real assholes in my life. What is that
I feel.

                    JEROME JR.
Girl you have tears in your eyes,
looking all sexy and holding me tight,
and showing me how much you love me.
You know what that is!!

Buzz

                    JEROME JR. (CONT'D)
All Dam, who could that be?

                    COOKIE
Probably your brother and Kathy.

Mason comes through the door not saying a word,
but doing the wonder dance Jerome join him,
Cookie and Kathy watching and laughing.

                    MASON
Congratulations my Brother, did you
call dad?

                    JEROME JR.
Not yet. (Ring) It's dad - hello.

                    JEROME SR.
What going on wonder man?

                    JEROME JR.
You saw it?

                    JEROME SR.
Son it brought tears to my eyes, seeing
our dance bringing people together;
It's a beautiful thing to see!

                    SNOOPY
          (Talking to Roscoe and Bryan) Looks
          like we got him on our team just in
          time. We are getting ready to explode!!

That guy Donald will be back Friday. We will
celebrate with him after the show. Just to show
our support.

FRIDAY NIGHT AFTER THE SHOW: SNOOPY MEETS DONALD
AND RICO.

Paul has changed Rico's look to the point Jerome
didn't know who he was. Donald and Jerome go's
upstairs before the second show to go over there
plans.

                    JEROME JR.
          Frank have you seen Rico? He would
          normally be here, - is this the
          undercover cop I will be working with?

                    RICO
          Yes Jerome, I'm the man!

                    JEROME JR.
          'Rico' man that guy is good, I can't
          believe It's you! When Donald and I
          introduce you to Snoopy - He will
          never know what happen.

Franks is packed for the second show. Snoopy and
his entourage are being seated.

                    SNOOPY
          'Wow' there's a lot of celebrities in
          hear tonight. There's Jerome and Donald,
          I guess the other guy is his Friend.

JEROME JR.
Do you like the name Melvin?

DONALD
Melvin sounds good to me.

JEROME JR.
Let's go introduce Melvin to Snoopy and
I want you to set with them through the
Show. Just make them feel comfortable.

As they are walking toward Snoopy, He's stopped
by Jimmy Felon.

JIMMY
Please give me a call, I want you to
come on my show and teach me your
dance.

JEROME JR.
Yes! I must tell you, you are one of my
favorites, I love watching your show.
Please meet with me after the show.
I have to introduce these guys to my
man, and then get ready to perform.

JIMMY
Sounds great, see you after the show.

JEROME JR.
Snoopy, you already know Donald, and
this is Melvin. Is it okay for them to
set with you guys: so y'all can get to
know each other.

                    SNOOPY
Of course, and tell that waitress to
bring two more glasses and we will see
you after the show.

Jerome tell the waitress to take more glasses to
Snoopy's table. Then gets ready to perform.

                    FRANK
He really don't need an introduction,
The world knows him now as the 'Wonder
man' come on put your hands together
for that man.

Everybody was saying in unison: Jerome's in house,
as he comes out dancing.

                RICO AS MELVEN
Man this guy is amazing!

                    SNOOPY
Wait till you hear him do stand up.

                RICO AS MELVEN
I heard he was funny, but when Jimmy
Fallon approached us, I almost peed
on myself.

They all laughed.

                    SNOOPY
I Know you didn't make that drive for
nothing.

                    DONALD
No I didn't, your product is really
good. As you know I own a clothing

store. This is my main man: he has had my back for 10 years, and you can trust him!

                    SNOOPY
Looking around at his gang - I'm okay with Melvin! Are you going to do business tonight?

                    DONALD
Yes, we're leaving early in the morning. I want to get about 50 thousand tonight for my immediate friend and Melvin is coming back next week to get no less than 200 thousand. Can you handle that?

                    SNOOPY
I will have whatever you need!

                    DONALD
That sounds good to me. When can I get what I want tonight.

                    SNOOPY
You said 50 right?

                    DONALD
Yes!

                    SNOOPY
Dennis go with Gary to get that and text me when you're on your way back: Donald and Jerome will meet you out side.

                    DENNIS
Okay, will do!

Twenty minutes later they meet out side and make the exchange.

                    DONALD
          Okay Guys I will see you next week, no
          I mean Melvin will see you.

                    GARY
          I was getting ready to say: but We will
          be waiting!

                    JEROME JR.
          I can't leave right now, Jimmy Fallon
          wants to talk to me about coming on
          his Show.

                    RICO AS MELVEN
          Did I hear you right: Jimmy Fallon want
          to talk to you?

                    JEROME JR.
          Didn't you see me talking to him?

                    RICO AS MELVEN
          Yeah, but I didn't know what it was
          about! - You know I'm your body guard
          right?

                    JEROME JR.
          Man you are the one that made all
          this happen, you can be my agent, body
          guard.

                    (MORE)

                    JEROME JR. (CONT'D)
You make your own title. (Looking him in
the eyes) Rico we are friend for life.

                    RICO AS MELVEN
Thanks for saying that, I even told
your brother: that you and I have
become more like brother, so I feel
the same way.

They go back inside; Jimmy sees Jerome approaching
him stand up and meet him with a big smile and a
hand shake to them.

                        JIMMY
Thank you for coming over, you and
your friend, come have a seat with us.

Donald can't believe he just shook Jimmy's hand.

                        DONALD
Jimmy forgive me if I get a little
emotional but, I have been a fan from
the first night they aired your show,
and to be setting at the same table
with you, wait until I tell my mother,
she's a big fan too.

                        JIMMY
If Jerome agree to come on my show:
you can bring your whole family and I
would love to meet your mother.

                    JEROME JR.
What do you mean if I agree - just let
me know when!

                    JIMMY
We're getting ready to start our new
season and you can be the first. We
start taping next week, can you make it.

                  JEROME JR.
(Singing) I'm already there!

They all laughed and talked until closing, as they
are leaving - Jimmy turns to Jerome.

                    JIMMY
I can count on you, Right?

                  JEROME JR.
I told you, I'm already there. But yes,
I will come up with Grady.

                    JIMMY
Yes! I didn't thank about that, so
we're all set. I'm excited - I'm going
to be practicing on them moves.

                  JEROME JR.
You can't be more excited then I am.
You have one of the biggest names in
late night TV, and you're inviting me
to come on your show!? I'm excited.

                    JIMMY
I'm flying out in the morning, and I
will see you next week.

They shake hands and say good buys.

DONALD
(With excitement in his voice) I can't
believe what just happen!

JEROME JR.
Me either, my girl is not going to
believe this. - I just thought about
next week.

RICO AS MELVEN
If you are thinking about Snoopy, we
can set up something before you leave.

JEROME JR.
Okay we will do that, it's still hard
to believe that's you! Have Lisa saw
you in your disguise.

RICO AS MELVEN
No, but my daughter is going to spend
the weekend with her cousin. After we
meet with Snoopy, I'm going to call her
and tell her that a friend of mine is
in town on a business trip, and he want
to see me before he leaves. I will tell
her to entertain him, well not really
entertain him!

JEROME JR.
I know what you mean, Just show some
hospitality!

RICO AS MELVEN
Yeah, that's what I'm talking about.!, I
will be home around four. I'm going to
see if she's as faithful as she claim
to be!

                    JEROME JR.
Well - no one will have to tell you,
you will know first hand! What if
she give in - (laughing), cause Paul
made you look better than Rico, I'm
just saying: you look pretty hot there
brother!

                  RICO AS MELVEN
That makes it even better!

WHEN HE COME CRYING: EVENING

Jerome is in New York with Jimmy Felon. Melvin
meets with Snoopy, then he decided to play a trick
on Lisa.

                      LISA
     (Ring ring) Hi honey.

                  RICO AS MELVEN
Hey babe, a friend of mine call me and
told me that his flight is going to
be held over for at least 3 hours. I
gave him our address, I don't mean to
put you on the spot but I want be home
until four.

                      LISA
Okay, what's your friend name?

                  RICO AS MELVEN
Melvin, okay sweetheart I have to go.

                      LISA
Did he give you a time?

RICO AS MELVEN

I don't know if he's coming - I'm just
giving you a heads up just in case he
do come by.

LISA

Okay I will be ready for whatever, I
love you and I will see you around
four, bye.

RICO AS MELVEN

I love you too, bye.

Twenty minutes later Melvin rings the door bell.
Lisa opens the door, the first thing she notice
was the bracelet she bought him. She then notice
other little things that made her know that was
her husband trying to play a trick on her.

LISA

Hi, you must be Melvin?

The first thing Lisa notice was the initialized
bracelet she bought him for his birthday, and
remembered him telling her about a makeup artist
and decided to play along not knowing where it
might end.

RICO AS MELVEN

Yes, 'wow' you have a beautiful home!

LISA

Thank you, will you excuse me for a
few minutes, I have to call a friend
of mine, I'll be right back.

She go's and call Jerome.

                    JEROME JR.
          (Ring ring) Lisa what's up?

                    LISA
          Your friend has disguised himself, I
          don't know who he suppose to be, but
          he say has name is Melvin. Do you know
          anything about this?

                    JEROME JR.
          No I don't. Are you sure it's him?

                    LISA
          I'm so sure it's him, if he make a move
          on me I'm going to give him some, and
          when he come crying to you, saying
          that I am a whore: show him this text
          that I'm going to send you. At least
          he will know that I knew it was him.
          I have to go!

Lisa sent Jerome a text saying "He forgot to
take off the bracelet I bought him for his
birthday. But when she returns she notice he has
removed it.

                    LISA (CONT'D)
          Sorry about that, can I get you
          something to drink?

                    RICO AS MELVEN
          Yes I will have a glass of wine. Can I
          use your rest room?

                    LISA
Sure, down the hall to your right?
(Lisa is doing all she can to keep from
laughing).

Melvin comes out of the bath room staring at Lisa.

                    LISA (CONT'D)
Is everything all right?

                    RICO AS MELVEN
Yeah, - I'm sorry for staring but you
are a beautiful woman!

                    LISA
Thank you, and you are a handsome man!

They are starring in each others eyes

                    RICO AS MELVEN
It's hard not to stare at you. - I'm
game if you are!

                    LISA
I thank you better leave, I don't know
what it is about you, but - I don't
know.

                    RICO AS MELVEN
What time is Rico coming home?

                    LISA
He told me around four.

                    RICO AS MELVEN
We have a whole hour, and I guarantee
you, you're going to love what I'm
going to do to you!

                    LISA
You sound pretty confident - I love my
husband!

When she said that, he felt real happy inside in
the sense that his wife is faithful.

                  LISA (CONT'D)
But, what he don't know want hurt him!

He's trying to play it off, but he can't believe
what he's hearing.

                 RICO AS MELVEN
You mean you're going to give me some?

                    LISA
Are we talking about the same thing? -
you said, I'm going to love what you're
going to put on me. What were you talking
about? Maybe I misunderstood you.

                 RICO AS MELVEN
I was talking about sex, I just didn't
think you would do it.

                    LISA
Well, you got me all horny talking
about, how I would love what you're
going to do to me. I want to see what
you got. (Looking down between his
legs) I can see you are getting a
little aroused. So I'm going to put on
a skirt, just in case he comes home
earlier than he said.

She leaves the room, and Rico's head is spinning.

                    RICO AS MELVEN
          (Talking to himself) How can she do
          this to me?

Lisa returns wearing a skirt, and pulling it up as
she approaches him, and bends over in front of him.

                    LISA
          Will you gently bite my butt cheeks,
          then pick me up, and slam me against
          the wall, and give me a moment I want
          forget.

He bite her butt cheeks. - Then picks her up, and
lay it on her. Lisa is screaming, as with total
ecstasy. But Rico has tears in his eyes, thinking
who is this woman I've been married to for 20
years. When they are done.

                    LISA (CONT'D)
          Oh my god that was so good!! I just
          hope he don't want to do anything when
          get home. I think I will tell him you
          never showed up. Because I need some
          time to recuperate.

                    RICO AS MELVEN
          (Nodding his head) yeah I should leave,
          I can't face him now. - I feel terrible
          for doing that to my friend.

                    LISA
          Dose that mean we can't have a secret
          affair.

                    JEROME JR.
Calling Rico

                  RICO AS MELVEN
(Ring ring) Rico, what up?

                    JEROME JR.
I - you must be still with Lisa as
Melvin.

                  RICO AS MELVEN
Yes, and you're not going to believe
what happen.

                    JEROME JR.
Can you pick me up from the airport
around noon tomorrow.

                  RICO AS MELVEN
Yeah, I will see you tomorrow. (Turns
to Lisa) sorry about that, anyway I
better leave.

                      LISA
You don't seem to be happy about what
we did.

                  RICO AS MELVEN
I'm not, Rico is a good man. That night
we met he spoke so highly of you.

                      LISA
You should have thought about that
before you got me all excited. But,
okay it was nice meeting, and screwing
you. It was really good!

He stares at her and leaves. About 30 minutes later he returns as Rico trying to act normal.

                    RICO
Hey babe, hugs, and kisses her. (While holding her) how was your day.

                    LISA
(Put her arms around his waist, laying her head on his chest with a smile on her face). My day was wonderful, and your friend - what was his name?

                    RICO
Melvin, did he...

                    LISA
He never showed up - and why is this my first time hearing about 'Melvin'!!

                    RICO
I was totally surprised to hear from him.

                    LISA
Who is he, and where did you meet him?

                    RICO
Clearing his throat, where did I meet? Oh, remember when the guys and I went deer hunting?

                    LISA
Yes I do.

                    RICO
That night we stop at a bar to have a
burger, and a beer. Melvin was shooting
pool by himself. I said do you want
competition? He said bring it on. I
invited him to come, and sit with us;
we exchanged numbers, and that was the
first, and last time we met.

                    LISA
(Trying to sound angry) That's my
point, -

                    RICO
(Looking shocked) What is your point?

                    LISA
...Your going to call me, and tell me
to entertain someone whom I've never
met. You've only met him once!! What if
he was a serial killer, and you came
home, and found me dead!?

Feeling like trash.

                    RICO
But honey, He didn't show up.

                    LISA
How do you know that? I could be...

                    RICO
Wait a minute, did he come by?

                    LISA
     (Quickly says) No, and I'm going to get
     a shower, and don't fellow me. Because
     I'm not in the mood.

Rico laps his forehead

                    RICO
     Honey I'm...

She walks away while he's talking, showers, and
go's to bed to watch Jerome on the Jimmy felon
show. After taking a shower Rico comes to bed.

                RICO (CONT'D)
     Honey I'm sorry I wasn't thinking, can
     I make it up to you!

                    LISA
     Yeah, you can leave your credit card
     when you leave in the morning.

                    RICO
     You mean I can't get some of that?
     (Putting his hands on her)

                    LISA
     (Moves his hands) I told you I am not
     in the mood! I have seen Jerome dance
     so I'm going to sleep, good night.

Rico is laying there thinking about how she made
love to Melvin. Tears running down the side of
his face. Lisa has her back to him with a smile
on her face.

SHE KNEW IT WAS YOU: NEXT DAY

As they are riding from the airport Jerome notice
how quiet Rico is.

                    JEROME JR.
     Is everything all right?

                    RICO
     Hell no! - My wife is a whore, I couldn't
     believe how she, - for instance she
     said I'm going to put on a skirt, just
     in case 'he', not my husband but just
     in case 'he' comes home earlier than
     he said.

                    JEROME JR.
     Laughing, I could have fun with this,
     but she knew it was you!

                    RICO
     No she didn't!

                    JEROME JR.
     Yes she did: read this! (Gives Rico
     his phone).

                    RICO
     (Reading out loud) Tell your friend
     he forgot to take off the bracelet I
     bought him for his birthday).

Then he started to laugh uncontrollably; man shes
really good. She played me like a flute!!!

JEROME JR.
Now that you know she played you, Lets focus on taking Snoopy down. Now when we meet this week I'm going to ask Bryan and Roscoe to ride with us. I'm going to be wired, I want you, to ask me to stop at a store.

While you're in the store; I'm going to try, and get them to confess to killing Cookie's parent's. Their thinking big money now: and I'm the source. So I believe one of them will talk!

LET'S TAKE HIS ASS DOWN: NIGHT

They meet with Snoopy one more time to buy a huge amount of the good stuff. They walk through the door.

SNOOPY
My man Jerome and I hope I'm getting it right, Melvin?

RICO AS MELVEN
That right.

SNOOPY
...and your friend Donald, tell him I'm coming to Florida next week, I want to check out that man bag he's selling. But I know you're here for business: so how much do you want?

RICO AS MELVEN
I hope you can handle this. Maybe we should have called. I won't be coming

back for at least two week. I have a bag in the car with $200.000 in it: can you do it?

                    SNOOPY
I - I should be able to do half of that.

                    RICO AS MELVEN
Well, I can only get what you got.

                    SNOOPY
I would rather you leave the money here. Bryan and Roscoe will take you to get it.

                    RICO AS MELVEN
Jerome will you get that bag out of your trunk?

Jerome go's and returns with the bag. Melvin gives him a 100.000. Then they leave, while riding along...

                    RICO AS MELVEN (CONT'D)
Jerome will you stop at the next store you see.

                    JEROME JR.
Is that quick and go okay?

                    RICO AS MELVEN
That will be perfect.

He pulls in and parks, Melvin go's into the store. While setting in the car.

                    JEROME JR.
You know we have been riding high for
three months. I don't know Melvin that
well but Donald and I are getting
ready to do something that will take
us over the top! But to honest, I don't
know if I can trust you guy's.

                    BRYAN
You know you can trust us!

                    JEROME JR.
Really? I lost two years of my life,
I know the both you had something to
do with it. If you just come clean,
maybe I can forgive you, but if you
keep acting like nothing ever happen,
tonight will be our last time doing
business with Snoopy.

                    BRYAN
Okay, - this is...

                    ROSCOE
Shut up Bryan!

                    BRYAN
The guy need to know what happen,
Snoopy told...

Roscoe pulls his gun out and put it to Bryan's
head.

                    ROSCOE
I told you to shut up, I'm not going
down like this.

> JEROME JR.

Man put the gun down, I'm not trying to find out who kill them, I just want to know how I got framed. This is what I do remember: I left with you guys, then waking up confused, and the Police pointing there guns telling me to drop my gun.

> ROSCOE

Okay Snoopy gave me a syringe and I stuck you in the neck and you were out for about 20 minutes.

> JEROME JR.

So one of you killed her parents.

> ROSCOE

I'm done talking!

Melvin is listening to every word, he calls his unit to come and surround the car.

> JEROME JR.

What the hell is going on?

Melvin come back to the car.

> RICO AS MELVEN

Jerome I am sorry, but I'm an under cover cop, and I budded your car and you guys will be put away for a long time. Please don't try to pull out your gun, because it won't be pretty.

The unit go's to Snoopy's, the swat team has surrounded his place with snipers. Dennis sees them on the surveillance, run to Snoopy.

                    DENNIS
     Hey boss we are being surrounded by
     the police.

                    SNOOPY
     'What' - everyone go to there hiding
     place.

They all had their own spot hollowed out behind the curtain that fits them perfectly. But what they didn't know is one of the snipers could see through a crack in the curtains on the window and saw Snoopy go behind the curtain.

                    RICO AS MELVEN
     Walks in with gun drown...

                    OFFICER TIM
     Rico get out of that room right now!!

Rico leaves the room.

                    RICO AS MELVEN
     Talk to me!

                    OFFICER TIM
     I don't know where the others went
     but your man is behind that curtain
     to your right as you walk in. I don't
     know if it leads to a tunnel, because
     I don't see any movement.

Oh wait a minute I think I saw some movement.

                    RICO AS MELVEN
What do you want me to do?

                    OFFICER TIM
Look and see if there are curtains
hanging in unusual places.

                    RICO AS MELVEN (CONT'D)
(Looking in) 'Wow' yeah I see four that
looks out of place.

                    OFFICER TIM
Okay, here's what I want you to do. I
want you to say allowed, as you are
walking toward the window. Where in
the hell can they be!? Then open the
curtains so I can see all four of them
and leave the room, I'm going to shoot
low, if they are lucky they might lose
a knee.

Rico dose what the officer says and leaves the
room.

                    RICO
You know Snoopy is a midget so shoot
real low.

                    OFFICER TIM
I saw the direction Snoopy went in, so
I'm going to see who's behind curtain
number one.

Officer Tim fire's a shot hitting Dennis In the
leg. Falls from behind the curtain, screaming
to the top of his voice. The others didn't hear

the firing of the gun, all they hear is Dennis screaming. They all stick their heads out to see what was going on. The Officer took them down one by one.

Then Rico and the other police rushed inn with guns drown.

                    SNOOPY
     'Melvin', what the hell?

                    RICO AS MELVEN
     My name is not Melvin, I'm an uncover
     cop who have been watching you for
     a long time, and it looks like greed
     wins again!

Rico go's home as Melvin, Lisa is laughing.

                    LISA
     Melvin I was hoping you would come
     back. (Before he says anything she give
     him a passionate kiss).

His daughter has never seen him as Melvin, but running in and seeing her mother kissing another man.

                    DAUGHTER
     I going to tell my dad, and runs back
     to her room.

                    RICO AS MELVEN
     I will handle this. (Go's to her room)
     Sweetheart.

                    DAUGHTER
          She recognized his voice, and turned
          facing him.

                    RICO AS MELVEN
          Honey this is dad, sometimes my job
          requires me to change my look, and I
          was playing with your mom but she knew
          it was me. I going to take this off,
          it looks kind of creepy but here I go.

After he removes it she jumps in his arms and
they laughed.

                    COOKIE
          (Ring ring) hello darling.

                    JEROME JR.
          We got his ass, and I'm going to call
          Mason and

                    COOKIE
          They are already here.

                    JEROME JR.
          Okay we're on our way!

When they get there: Jerome comes in doing the
dance and they all joined in, even Rico tried to
do the dance. They all laughed at him.

                    JEROME JR.
          Mason, can I see you in the other room
          for a minute?

                    MASON
Yeah, what's up?

                  JEROME JR.
I'm going to propose to Cookie.

                    MASON
Man, that is exactly what I was
thinking, but I was waiting until you
got here.

                  JEROME JR.
Well, let's go and do this.

They come out of the room dancing. Jerome takes
Cookie by the hand, and Melvin takes Kathy by
the hand.

                    LISA
Knowing what they are going do, is
so excited. Put her arm around Rico,
honey, can you believe this. They both
are going to propose.

                    RICO
Yes, and I am so happy for them,
especially Jerome, my little Brother.

They both kneel on one knee, they said at the
same time. Will you marry me? Cookie and Kathy
said yes, at the same time. The girls got pregnant
in the same month. They both had boys. Jerome
Jr. the 2nd and Mason Jr. Before they could walk,
when they hear music, they would be moving their
little feet and hands.

                    JEROME JR.
Hey, brother do your son have the
rhythm already? Because when I turn
on the music: this boy is moving with
the music.

                    MASON
Yes! I was blown away! The other day I
was listening to some music: Jerome,
I'm not lying this boy was moving with
the beat.

Six years later, they are now in school. The
teachers knows, what Jerome Jr. did. Taking down
the notorious drug dealer, Snoopy and his gang.
So when Jerome would come to class, everyone,
including the teacher. Saying, Jerome's in the
house. His Brother Mason, not saying a word, but
dancing like his brother. It ends with both of
them with one foot in the air. The End.

(CONT'D)

(CONT'D)